A Scientific Autobiography

OPPOSITIONS BOOKS

Postscript by Vincent Scully
Translation by Lawrence Venuti

Aldo Rossi

A Scientific Autobiography

Published for The Graham Foundation for Advanced Studies
in the Fine Arts, Chicago, Illinois, and
The Institute for Architecture and Urban Studies,
New York, New York, by

The MIT Press
Cambridge, Massachusetts, and London, England

1981

Sixth printing, 1992
First paperback printing, 1984

Copyright © 1981 by
The Institute for Architecture and
Urban Studies and
The Massachusetts Institute of
Technology

*Library of Congress Cataloguing in
Publication Data*
Rossi, Aldo, 1931–
A scientific autobiography.
"Published for the Graham
Foundation for Advanced Studies in
the Fine arts, Chicago, Illinois, and
the Institute for Architecture and
Urban Studies, New York,
New York."
1. Rossi, Aldo, 1931–.
2. Architects—Italy—Biography.
3. Architecture—Philosophy.
I. Title. II. Series.
NA1123.R616A2 1981
720′.92′4 [B]   81-17164
ISBN 0-262-18104-5 (H) AACR2
      0-262-68041-6 (P)

This book was set in VIP Century
Expanded by DEKR Corporation
and printed and bound by Halliday
Lithograph Corporation in the
United States of America.

*Cover drawing: Guarino Guarini,
Architettura Civile, Plate 38*

Other Titles in the OPPOSITIONS
BOOKS series:

**Essays in Architectural Criticism:
Modern Architecture and
Historical Change**
Alan Colquhoun
Preface by Kenneth Frampton

The Architecture of the City
Aldo Rossi
Introduction by Peter Eisenman
Translation by Diane Ghirardo and
Joan Ockman

Contents

I felt that the disorder of things, if limited and somehow honest, might best correspond to our state of mind.

But I detested the arbitrary disorder that is an indifference to order, a kind of moral obtuseness, complacent well-being, forgetfulness.

To what, then, could I have aspired in my craft?

Certainly to small things, having seen that the possibility of great ones was historically precluded.

I began these notes about ten years ago, and I am trying to conclude them now so that they do not turn into memories. From a certain point in my life, I considered craft or art to be a description of things and of ourselves; for this reason, I have always admired Dante's *Commedia*, which begins when the poet is around thirty years old. By thirty, one ought to have completed or begun something definitive, and come to terms with one's own formation. All my drawings and writings have seemed to me definitive in two ways: first, they concluded my experience, and second, I then had nothing more to say.

Every summer seemed to me my last summer, and this sense of stasis without evolution may explain many of my projects. Nonetheless, to understand or explain my architecture, I must again run through things and impressions, must again describe them, or find a way to do so.

Certainly a very important point of reference is Max Planck's *Scientific Autobiography*. In this book, Planck returns to the discoveries of modern physics, recapturing the impression made on him by the enunciation of the principle of the conservation of energy; he always recalled this principle in connection with his schoolmaster Mueller's story about a mason who with great effort heaved a block of stone up on the roof of a house. The mason was struck by the fact that expended energy does not get lost; it remains stored for many years, never diminished, latent in the block of stone, until one day it happens that the block slides off the roof and falls on the head of a passerby, killing him.

It may seem strange that Planck and Dante associate their scientific and autobiographical search with death, but it is a death that is in some sense a continuation of energy. Actually, the principle of the conservation of energy is mingled in every artist or technician with the search for happiness and death. In architecture this search is also undoubtedly bound up with the material and with energy; and if one fails to take note of this, it is not possible to comprehend any building, either from a technical point of view or from a compositional one. In the use of every material there must be an anticipation of the construction of a place and its transformation.

The double meaning of the Italian word *tempo*, which signifies both atmosphere and chronology, is a principle that presides over every construction; this is the double meaning of energy that I now see clearly in architecture, as well as in other technics or arts. In my first book, *The Architecture of the City*, I identified this precise problem with the relation between form and function: form persists and comes to preside over a built work in a world where functions continually become modified; and in form, material is modified. The material of a bell is transformed into a cannon ball; the form of an amphitheater into that of a city; the form of a city into a palace. Written when I was close to thirty, this book seemed definitive to me, and even today its theses have yet to be sufficiently extended. Later I clearly saw that the work should have encompassed a more comprehensive set of themes, especially in light of the analogies which intersect all of our actions.

Ever since my first projects, where I was interested in purism, I have loved contaminations, slight changes, self-commentaries, and repetitions.

1. "Sacri Monti were characteristic developments of Mannerist piety in Lombardy—sequences of chapels housing representations of incidents in some sacred story, to be visited by pilgrims in their narrative order and culminating, at the highest point of the processional way, in some such feature as a reproduction of the Holy Sepulchre. These [were] unique combinations of architecture and landscape perambulation." Anna Tomlinson, "Sacri Monti," *The Architectural Review*, vol. 116, December 1954.

My early education was not exactly in the visual arts, and in any case, even today I think that one craft has the same value as another, provided it has a precise goal. I could have done anything, and in fact my interest and activity in architecture began rather late. Actually, I believe that I have always been attentive to forms and things, but at the same time I have always regarded them as the final moment of a complex system, of an energy which only became visible through these facts. Thus in my childhood I was particularly struck by the Sacri Monti:[1] I felt certain that sacred history was completely summed up in the plaster figure, in the motionless gesture, in the expression stopped in the course of a story that would otherwise have been impossible to tell.

This is the very principle that appears in Renaissance treatises with reference to the medieval masters: the description and the prominence accorded to the ancient forms permitted a continuity which otherwise could not have been maintained, as well as a transformation, once life was fixed in precise forms. I was amazed by Alberti's persistence, at Rimini and Mantua, in repeating the forms and spaces of Rome, as if a contemporary history did not exist; in fact, he worked scientifically with the only material possible and available to an architect. Just standing in Sant'Andrea at Mantua I had this first impression of the relation between *tempo*, in its double atmospheric and chronological sense, and architecture; I saw the fog enter the basilica, as I often love to watch it penetrate the Galleria in Milan: it is the unforeseen element that modifies and alters, like light and shadow, like stones worn smooth by the feet and hands of generations of men.

Perhaps this alone was what interested me in architecture: I knew that architecture was made possible by the confrontation of a precise form with time and the elements, a confrontation which lasted until the form was destroyed in the process of this combat. Architecture was one of the ways that humanity had sought to survive; it was a way of expressing the fundamental search for happiness.

This search still excites me in archaeological collections, in clay material, in tools, in fragments where the ancient stone is confounded with bone and where the structure of the skeleton is lost in that bone. As a result, I love museums of paleontology and those patient reconstructions of fragments without significance into the significance of form. This love for the fragment and for the thing binds us to apparently insignificant objects, and we attribute to them the same importance that we customarily give to art.

I have always had a strong interest in objects, instruments, apparatus, tools. Without intending to I used to linger for hours in the large kitchen at S., on Lake Como, drawing the coffeepots, the pans, the bottles. I particularly loved the strange shapes of the coffeepots enameled blue, green, red; they were miniatures of the fantastic architectures that I would encounter later. Today I still love to draw these large coffeepots, which I liken to brick walls, and which I think of as structures that can be entered.

This interior-exterior aspect of architecture was certainly first suggested to me by the San Carlone at Arona, a work which I have drawn and studied so many times that it is now difficult for me to relate it to the visual education of my childhood. I subsequently understood that it pleased me because here the limits that distinguish the domains of architecture, the machine, and instruments were dissolved in marvelous invention. As with the Homeric horse, the pilgrim enters the body of the saint as he would a tower or a wagon steered by a knowing technician. After he mounts the exterior stair of the pedestal, the steep ascent through the interior of the body reveals the structure of the work and the welded seams of the huge pieces of sheet metal. Finally, he arrives at the interior-exterior of the head; from the eyes of the saint, the view of the lake acquires infinite contours, as if one were gazing from a celestial observatory.

But perhaps the very dimensions of this construction give me a strange feeling of happiness: its strength is potential. When one observes a motionless locomotive or tank, the effect is not very different.

This first impression of the interior-exterior aspect has become clear more recently, at least as a problem: if I relate it to the coffeepots, it is also bound up with food and with the objects in which food is cooked; the true meaning of the manufacture of utensils and pots, which often, annoyingly, is obscured when they are accumulated and displayed in museums, is something that is continually presented to us.

I possess a strange photograph of a face behind the grate of a castle or a convent. From the photograph it is difficult to know whether one is seeing from the point of view of the person who looks at us or from the opposite side. Examining this photo I do not so much pose for myself the banal problem of how this effect might be, so to speak, expressible in architecture, or even in film or in some other medium; but rather I realize how the grate is the means which makes the occurrence possible: in this case, the appearance of the young man's face. By a singular coincidence, sometime after I first saw this photograph, I visited the cells of the sisters in the Convent of Las Pelayas at Santiago de Compostela, and I again saw the effect that had been captured in the photograph. The facade of Las Pelayas is one of the masterworks of seventeenth-century Spanish architecture, and it had always made such a strong impression on me that Catalan friends, in one of their publications, treated it as an image analogous to my building in the Gallaratese quarter of Milan. There, in the interior of the cells, I noted a striking luminosity which contradicted the nearly prison-like aspect of the exterior facade. The same shouts that reached the outside of the convent were perceived on the inside with even greater sharpness, as in a theater. In the same way the young man's eyes perceive the sight of the exterior as in a theater, or as one who watches a performance.

Similarly, architecture becomes the vehicle for an event we desire, whether or not it actually occurs; and in our desiring it, the event becomes something "progressive" in the Hegelian sense. I shall come back to this later. But it is for this reason that the dimensions of a table or a house are very important— not, as the functionalists thought, because they carry out a determined function, but because they permit other functions.

Finally, because they permit everything that is unforseeable in life.

In my interest for objects, I must admit that I have always managed to confuse the thing itself with the word through a kind of ignorance, or prejudice, or even through the suspension that this could give to the meaning of a statement or a drawing.

For example, I have always conceived of the term "apparatus" (*apparecchio*) in a rather singular way: it is related to my reading and possession in early youth of the volume by Alfonso dei Liguori entitled *Apparecchio alla morte*. This strange book, which I still recall in many images, seemed to me to be an apparatus itself just by virtue of its rather small and very wide format: I felt that one need not even read the book because it was sufficient merely to own it; it was an instrument. But the connection between apparatus and death also reasserted itself in such common phrases as *apparecchiare la tavola*, meaning to set the table, to prepare it, to arrange it. From this point on I came to regard architecture as the instrument which permits the unfolding of a thing. I must say that over the years this awareness has increased my interest in my craft, especially in my latest projects, where I have tried to propose buildings which, so to speak, are vehicles for events. I shall talk later about some of these projects.

I can say now that they achieve a silence, a degree of silence which is different from the purism I had striven for in my early designs, where I was concerned primarily with light, walls, shadows, openings. I have realized that it is impossible to recreate an atmosphere. Things are better experienced and then abandoned; initially, everything should be foreseeable, even though what is not foreseeable is all the more fascinating because it remains beyond us.

Finally, from my childhood education I cannot forget the Sacri Monti of S. that I mentioned before and the other Sacri Monti that we visited at the shores of lakes. Undoubtedly, they gave me my first contact with figurative art, and I was, as I now am, attracted by stasis and naturalness, by the classicism of architecture and by the naturalism of people and objects. The quality of suspension that I experienced in them aroused in me forms of exalted coolness; here too I wanted to pass beyond the window grate, to set out one of my own objects on the tablecloth used at the last meal, to escape the condition of a passerby. In all of my projects and drawings, I believe there may be a hint of this naturalism which transcends their oddities and defects. When I saw the complete work of Edward Hopper in New York, I realized all this about my architecture: paintings like *Chair Car* or *Four Lane Road* took me back to the stasis of those timeless miracles, to tables set for eternity, drinks never consumed, things which are only themselves.

In thinking of these works, I notice that what interests me most are things which are about to be stated and the mechanism by which they might be stated, although I am also aware that another, more obscure mechanism tends to impede the normal completion of necessary operations so that something else may take place. This is connected with the problem of freedom; for me, freedom can also be translated into craft; I do not know exactly what kind of freedom is at issue here, but I have always found some means to defend it.

Of course, there are many examples of this freedom. Precisely because I am writing an autobiography of my projects which is mingled with my personal history, I certainly cannot avoid recalling the effect that *The Life of Henri Brulard* produced in me when I was a boy. It was perhaps through Stendhal's drawings and this strange mixture of autobiography and building plans that I acquired my first knowledge of architecture; they were the first seeds of a notion which ultimately ends up in this book. I was struck by the drawings of plans which seemed to be a graphic variation of the handwritten manuscript, and principally for two reasons: first, because handwriting is a complex technique that lies between writing and drawing—I shall return to this in relation to other experiences—and second, because these plans disregarded or ignored formal and dimensional aspects.

In some of my recent projects, or ideas for projects, I try to stop the event just before it occurs, as if the architect could foresee—and in a certain sense does foresee—the unfolding of life in the house. It is difficult for interior decorators to understand all this: they are caught up with ephemeral things like the design of the detail, the frame, things which in reality are replaced by the life of the house. Perhaps these same drawings of Stendhal later led me to the study of housing types and the fundamental nature of typology. It is curious that I began my academic career as a lecturer on the "functional aspects of buildings," a discipline now abolished, and that this fabric of distances and dimensions seemed to me the specter or skeleton of architecture. The plan became a physical condition, as when one passes through Ostia or any city where planimetric outlines are apparent; at first, there is a subtle disappointment, but then you slowly reconstruct the architecture so that it is possible to see what was a door, and a room, and a passageway where life formerly took place. It is said that years ago in Seville whoever had a house built instructed the architect, or simply the mason, what the dimensions of the patio should be, and then added that he should draw around it a possible configuration of rooms. This too seems to me connected with the problem of freedom and the imagination: since there are few things that are fixed, they cannot be miscalculated; they become the meaning of the building.

These observations are not intended to establish any sense of confidence in education; how we learn is also important. Certainly some things are unthinkable if they are not related to the emotions with which we first experienced them. There are some facts which are extremely important for me, especially from a formal point of view, but which are very difficult for me to communicate.

One morning, as I was passing through the Grand Canal in Venice on a *vaporetto*, someone suddenly pointed out to me Filarete's column and the Vicolo del Duca and the humble houses constructed where the ambitious palace of this Milanese lord was to have been. I always observe this column and its base, this column that is both a beginning and an end. This document or relic of time, in its absolute formal purity, has always seemed to me a symbol of architecture consumed by the life which surrounds it. I have rediscovered Filarete's column in the Roman ruins at Budapest, in the transformation of certain amphitheaters, and above all as one possible fragment of a thousand other buildings. Probably, too, I am fond of fragments for the same reason that I have always thought that it was good luck to meet a person with

6

*3 Convent of Las Pelayas, Santiago
de Compostela.*

whom one has broken ties: it shows confidence in a fragment of ourselves.

But the question of the fragment in architecture is very important since it may be that only ruins express a fact completely. Photographs of cities during war, sections of apartments, broken toys. Delphi and Olympia. This ability to use pieces of mechanisms whose overall sense is partly lost has always interested me, even in formal terms. I am thinking of a unity, or a system, made solely of reassembled fragments. Perhaps only a great popular movement can give us the sense of an overall design; today we are forced to stop ourselves at certain things. I am convinced, however, that architecture as totality, as a comprehensive project, as an overall framework, is certainly more important and, in the final analysis, more beautiful. But it happens that historical obstacles—in every way parallel to psychological blocks or symptoms—hinder every reconstruction. As a result, I believe that there can be no true compensation, and that maybe the only thing possible is the addition that is somewhere between logic and biography.

As I continue these autobiographical notes, I should speak of several projects which characterize certain moments in my life; they are well-known projects which I have always avoided discussing directly. The first is the project for the cemetery at Modena, the second the project for student housing at Chieti. I believe that the first, by its very theme, expresses the end both of adolescence and of an interest in death, while the second signifies a search for happiness as a condition of maturity. In neither project have I renounced the liturgical sense of architecture, meaning that I have not done much more than has already been established by convention, even though the results are quite singular. The first project is strongly bound up with certain experiences and with the conclusion of the search for fragments in the skeletal form. The second has to do with a state of happiness; it is like Christmas and, in another way, like Sunday. The quest for happiness is identified with the happy time of a holiday—especially because at such times, when things come to a halt, it seems impossible to withstand the force of happiness.

Nevertheless, I realized a great deal about these two projects in 1975, during the interval between them, when I designed the Palazzo della Ragione in Trieste. I perceived that I had simply recounted—in architecture and in writings—my impressions on certain mornings when I read the newspaper in the great *Lichthof* of the University of Zurich, whose roof resembles, unless I am mistaken, the pyramidal roof of the *Kunsthaus*. The *Lichthof* is a place that is very dear to me. Now, because of my interest in this place I asked Heinrich Helfenstein to photograph the interior, which is always full of students from the ground floor up through the successive levels. And what was undoubtedly a university I saw as a bazaar, teeming with life, as a public building or ancient bath.

Helfenstein took some very beautiful photographs of the *Lichthof*, but unlike my account of that place, his unique sensibility led him to take them during a holiday. In these photographs, the luminous court and the aerial galleries are absolutely empty, the building is uninhabited, and it is even difficult to comprehend how it might be inhabited. In fact, Helfenstein refused to rep-

5 *Filarete's Column, Venice.*

resent either the purity or the life of the *Lichthof*. He caught its potential for being lived in. These photographs *suspended* the life which the building could contain, and only by observing this suspension did I clearly see the palm trees in the glass-walled court, thus associating all this with the notion of a greenhouse, an enormous *Palmenhaus;* I connected the University with the Invernadero at Barcelona and with the gardens at Seville and Ferrara, where I experience a peace that is nearly complete.

But in depicting the two palms, the photographs reminded me of the facade of the Hotel Due Palme on Lake M., where I spend some of my time; the facade of the hotel constituted anew a sensitive manifestation of architecture, one that went beyond any stylistic or technical reference.

The significance of the operation was much richer than I thought it would be at the beginning. The very same thing happened when we designed a table *after* the project for the cemetery at Modena. This table was intended for an exhibition, but in designing it, we realized that we were abandoning our original path to follow a sort of compelling labyrinth. In fact, the labyrinth amused us because we found the goose game[2] in it, thinking to make the design simulate a children's game. But how could we not have recalled that the sinister element of this game, especially for children, is represented by the square of death? The subject of death was something that had automatically found its way into the process of designing. The project itself became a rediscovered object, an object of affection, as do all projects when they are redesigned. The two different models of the Segrate Monument are two different objects, and we expressed part of our affection for the smallest one by calling it, as we do in the studio, the "Segratino": this name indicates the individuality of that model, which is also, but not only, related to its scale and its material.

2. The labyrinth-like playing board for this game consists of sixty-three divisions painted in a spiral, with a goose depicted in every ninth space.

In April of 1971, on the road to Istanbul between Belgrade and Zagreb, I was involved in a serious auto accident. Perhaps as a result of this incident, the project for the cemetery at Modena was born in the little hospital of Slawonski Brod, and simultaneously, my youth reached its end. I lay in a small, ground-floor room near a window through which I looked at the sky and a little garden. Lying nearly immobile, I thought of the past, but sometimes I did not think: I merely gazed at the trees and the sky. This presence of things and of my separation from things—bound up also with the painful awareness of my own bones—brought me back to my childhood. During the following summer, in my study for the project, perhaps only this image and the pain in my bones remained with me: I saw the skeletal structure of the body as a series of fractures to be reassembled. At Slawonski Brod, I had identified death with the morphology of the skeleton and the alterations it could undergo. I now realize, however, that to regard death as a kind of fracture is a one-sided interpretation.

Having finished this project, I returned to Istanbul by car in the month of November. These two trips to Istanbul are like a continuation of the same project, and I often confuse the places. It is a matter of an interrupted journey. The principal place, I believe, consists of the green Mosque of Bursa, where I again felt a great passion for architecture, an interest which I rarely feel so strongly. In the mosque, I re-experienced a sensation which I had not felt since childhood: that of being invisible, of being on the other side of the spectacle in a certain sense. Because of this inability to live it fully, I have always thought that art, except in the theater, is never a satisfying experience. I believe that some of these motifs from the Turkish world recur in several of my subsequent drawings for the cemetery project. Yet their reappearance is also due to the fact that the principal problem had been dissolved, so to speak, along with the project itself. The sense of deposition corresponded with the form of the bone, which I have remarked on in other writings.

The deposition is not a typical theme in architecture, yet in the Slawonski Brod period, I attempted to represent a deposed form: for me, deposed architecture is only partially anthropomorphic. The Deposition from the Cross in painting, as in the works of Rosso Fiorentino and Antonello da Messina at the Prado, studies the mechanical possibilities of the body, and I have always thought that the theme succeeds in communicating to us a certain pathos through the abnormal position which a corpse assumes when it is carried. These positions may be related to erotic ones, yet they do not occur as a result of an internal movement, and furthermore, they represent everything that is object-like in the body. This quality of the body as object is particularly distressing and painful for the viewer, who relates the deposition to illness even more than to death. On the other hand, the deposition admits of a system, an edifice, a body, wanting at the same time to break that frame of reference and thereby compel us to see a different significance, which is certainly more disquieting by virtue of its impossibility.

From this arise superimpositions, changes, excavations of objects, identifications between various materials. One of a number of examples which confirms this thesis is to be found in the convent of Santa Clara at Santiago de Compostela.

Yet this first analysis of the project, already a descent into the Lombard world, was to my discomfort accompanied by literary and visual suggestions of certain leftist imitators of the writer Alessandro Manzoni—the romanticism of the excluded, of ancient courts and Milanese buildings, public places, exaggerated and almost infamous institutions, as in the Milan of Valera. The paintings of Angelo Morbelli, like *Il Natale dei remasti* and *Pio Albergo Trivulzio*, had always impressed me: I had observed them with fascination, not knowing how to judge them. Now they served me as the plastic and figurative means for this project. The study of light, the great bands of light that fall on the benches filled with old people, the precise shadows cast by the geometrical forms of these seats and by the stove, seem to be taken from a manual on the theory of shadow.

A diffuse luminosity pervades the large room, where the figures lose themselves as in a piazza. The practice of carrying naturalism to its extreme consequences leads to a kind of metaphysics of the object; things, old people's bodies, light, a cold ambience—all are offered through a kind of observation that seems distant. Yet this emotionless distance is precisely the deathly air of the poorhouse. When I was designing the cemetery at Modena, I constantly thought about this hospice, and the light which traces precise bands on that section of the painting is the same as that which passes through the windows of this project.

In the end the building became an abandoned one, a place where life stops,

12

6 Synagogue, Pesaro.

7 Lichthof, The University of Zurich. Photograph by Heinrich Helfenstein.

work is suspended, and the institution itself becomes uncertain. I remember how this project provoked ferocious attacks on me which I did not comprehend; attacks were even directed at my entire architectural activity.

Yet what had a greater impact on me was the critics' reduction of the project to a sort of neo-Enlightenment experiment. I believe that this reaction occurred above all because it was seen as a translation of the work of Etienne-Louis Boullée, not because of any critical intention.

In fact, as I now see it rising today, I find in this great house of the dead a living sense of *pietà*: just as in the Roman tomb of the baker. Thus, this house of the dead, constructed according to the rhythm of urban mortality itself, has a tempo linked to life, as all structures ultimately do.

Just as the structure itself has undergone modifications, so with slight variations its form recurs in many of my drawings. The slogan of the competition for which it was designed was "the blue of the sky," and now when I look at those huge, blue, sheet-metal roofs, so sensitive to day and evening light as well as to that of the seasons, they sometimes seem deep blue, sometimes the clearest azure. The pink stucco of the walls covers the Emilian brick of the old cemetery, and it too displays the effects of the light, appearing almost white or else dark pink.

Yet in the project this building already belonged to the great mists of the Po valley and to the deserted houses on the river bank, abandoned for years in the wake of the great floods. In these houses, one can still find broken cups, iron beds, shattered glass, yellowed photos, along with the dampness and other signs of the river's devastation. There are villages where the river appears with the continuity of death, leaving only signs, signals, fragments; yet they are fragments that one cherishes.

In Lisbon, there is a cemetery which is curiously called "the cemetery of pleasure," but no one has ever explained to me the origin of this name; in America, there are cemeteries as large as parks or suburbs. There are different customs and forms for the places of death as for those of life, but often we hardly grasp the boundary between the two conditions.

If I were to redo this project, perhaps I would do it exactly the same; perhaps I would redo all of my projects in the same way. Yet it is also true that everything that has happened is already history, and it is difficult to think that things could occur in any other way.

With this project, my meditation on architecture expanded, and gradually it seemed to me that I was better able to grasp a more distant time, that I could recognize in a drawing, a story, a novel, the threads which unite analysis with expression. Around 1960 I wrote *The Architecture of the City*, a successful book. At that time, I was not yet thirty years old, and as I have said, I wanted to write a definitive work: it seemed to me that everything, once clarified, could be defined. I believed that the Renaissance treatise had to become an apparatus which could be translated into objects. I scorned memories, and at the same time, I made use of urban impressions: behind feelings I searched for the fixed laws of a timeless typology. I saw courts and galleries, the elements of urban morphology, distributed in the city with the purity of mineralogy. I read books on urban geography, topography, and history, like a general who wishes to know every possible battlefield—the high grounds, the passages, the woods. I walked the cities of Europe to understand their plans and classify them according to types. Like a lover sustained by my egotism, I often ignored the secret feelings I had for those cities; it was enough to know the system that governed them. Perhaps I simply wanted to free myself of the city. Actually, I was discovering my own architecture. A confusion of courtyards, suburban houses, roofs, gas storage drums, comprised my first exploration of a Milan that seemed fantastic to me. The bourgeois world of villas by lakes, the corridors of the boarding school, the huge kitchens in country houses—these were memories of a landscape out of Manzoni which disintegrated in the city. Yet their insistence on things revealed a craft to me.

8 *Houses on a canal, Milan.*

I searched for it in history, and I translated it into my own history. Thus typological and functional certainty were extended, or brought back, to the world of objects: the house I designed at Borgo Ticino rediscovered the cabins of fishermen, the world of the lake and the river, a typology without history. I have seen these same houses in northern Portugal and in Galveston, Texas, on the coast of the Gulf of Mexico. By this point it seemed to me sufficient to fix upon objects, understand them, repropose them. Rationalism is necessary, like order, but whatever the order, it can be upset by the external factors of another order—whether historical, geological, psychological.

Thus the temporal aspect of architecture no longer resided in its dual nature of light and shadow or in the aging of things; it rather presented itself as a catastrophic moment in which time takes things back.

These thoughts have led me to the concept of identity.

And the loss of it. Identity is something unique, typical, but it is also a choice.

In several of my drawings, particularly *L'architecture assassinée* and *The Cabins of Elba*, as well as in others, I have tried to express these relations.

I revaluated the cabins, those little wooden constructions and their deformations: the world of the South from the Mediterranean to the Pacific.

In working on my project for the Corral del Conde I rediscovered all these implications at Seville. Seville lives the life of its two or more souls during Holy Week and the summer holidays. They are perhaps the greatest works of architecture I have known.

In *The Architecture of the City*, I spoke of the cities of Andalusia; buildings like the Alhambra in Granada and the Mezquita in Córdoba were the paradigms of an architecture which is transformed over time, of an architecture acquainted with immense spaces and delicate solutions and constituting the city. I now realize that these impressions are reflected in my architecture. The analogical links, the associations between things and situations, became

9 Houses on the delta of the Po
River.

multiplied during my stay in Andalusia, so that images of the structure of the house of Seville began to emerge elsewhere, mixing autobiography and civic history. I have always loved the typology of the corral and often proposed it in my work. The corral was the form of life in the houses of old Milan; it constituted the form of the country dairy farm and dates back to the Imperial agricultural villa which was enclosed like a little city at the end of the *Pax Romana*. I saw the corral in the old houses of Milan, together with the balcony which is closely related to it, as a form of life made up of the intimacies endured there, the bonds, the intolerances. In my bourgeois childhood, I felt excluded by these houses, and I entered the courtyards with curiosity and fear. Later, the scientific bent of my research estranged me from what was most important, namely the imagination of which such relations are made. This imagination rose up again in me in the corrals of Seville, in those larger and older corrals, in those very narrow ones with intersecting stairs and balconies, in the green cast-iron columns from the turn of the century— buildings still rich in imagination from the life of an urban proletariat.

It is certain that behind many of these structures we see the signs of ancient misery, and we would like to overturn them. Yet we must also take hold of these very dense images which will comprise the history of the new city.

For me, the architectural work is now identified with these things: there is a street in Seville made up of superimposed balconies, elevated bridges, stairs, noise, and silence, and it seems to recur in all my drawings. Here the search has ended; its object is the architecture it has rediscovered.

This rediscovered architecture is part of our civic history. All gratuitous invention is removed; form and function are by now identified in the object; the object, whether part of the country or the city, is a relationship of things. There no longer exists purity of design which is not also a recompositioning of all this, and in the end the artist can write, in Walter Benjamin's words, "Therefore I am deformed by connections with everything that surrounds me here."

The emergence of relations among things, more than the things themselves, always gives rise to new meanings.

At Córdoba, Juan Serrano presented me with a fantastic book which I have found most valuable for architecture, not for the architecture of Córdoba or Andalusia, but for comprehending the structure of the city. The title of the book is *Paseos por Córdoba*, and I believe it is not very well known. I have not termed this book fantastic by accident. In it the topographic reality, the typology of the dwellings, the very chronology itself, are continually inter- twined with emotion, anecdote, apparition, in such a way as to give us a time different from the one we know. In this long and very densely written volume, the city is analyzed or, better, searched out in its most unexpected dimensions, dimensions which the author often tries to relate to the urban question, apologizing all the while for the very detailed character of his research: "I hope my readers will forgive me if I occasionally digress from the subject of this book to discuss a term so common as the name of a street." Yet the subject of the book is construed precisely in terms of its internal relations, and the city that is rediscovered is ultimately identified with the autonomy of the researcher.

I wish only to emphasize how a building, how architecture may be a primary element onto which life is grafted. This idea, to which I return in my lectures, was made particularly clear to me by several "urban artifacts" at Seville, especially the enormous encampment of the summer holidays, rigorously laid out like a Roman city, with its lots divided into the minimal dimensions for the little houses, and with its huge triumphal portals. This encampment forms the weak but very precisely jointed skeleton of an unsettled and convulsive body, one that is destined to the short, intense life of the holidays.

I am not familiar with Holy Week in Seville, but in churches and museums I have seen the statues and the carts, the Virgins and the Christs, and these things too seem like the architectonic instruments of an action that is prearranged, yes, but still unforeseeable.

I have always believed that in life as in architecture, whenever we search for something, we do not find merely what we have sought; in every search there is always a degree of unforeseeability, a sort of troubling feeling at the conclusion. Thus the architect must prepare his instruments with the modesty of a technician; they are the instruments of an action which he can only glimpse, or imagine, although he knows that the instrument itself can evoke and suggest the action. I particularly love empty theaters with few lights lit and, most of all, those partial rehearsals where the voices repeat the same bar, interrupt it, resume it, remaining in the potentiality of the action. Likewise in my projects, repetition, collage, the displacement of an element from one design to another, always places me before another potential project which I would like to do but which is also a memory of some other thing.

Because of this, cities, even if they last for centuries, are in reality great encampments of the living and the dead where a few elements remain like signals, symbols, warnings. When the holiday is over, the elements of the architecture are in tatters, and the sand again devours the street. There is nothing left to do but resume, with persistence, the reconstruction of elements and instruments in expectation of another holiday.

When from a terrace on the Mincio River I looked at the remains of an old bridge, composed of simple iron and reinforcing beams, I saw the structure in all its clarity and the formal and technical analogies of the architecture. This analogous architecture brought back nature: it was like an illumination, perhaps only glimpsed for the first time. The pattern of the brick in the collapsed wall, the section revealed by the ruin of time, the iron shaped like beams, the water of the canal—all these things constituted this work.

The project was merely the pretext for a more general involvement: today I could not explain the many imitations of my work except in terms of this easily acquired ability to see.

Objects which are no longer usable become fixed in their last known gesture: in the analogical process, the abandoned houses virtually became subsumed as points of reference, conclusions of a hypothetical project that no longer would be possible for me to complete in any other way.

20

11 Bridge on the Mincio River.

It is no longer possible to do anything about it: to modify the misery of modern culture, a great popular movement is necessary, and the misery of architecture is the expression of this knowledge.

In looking at a ruin, especially in the city, I noticed that the contours of things became clouded and confusing. In the exaggerated silence of an urban summer, I grasped the deformation, not only of ourselves, but of objects and things as well. Perhaps there was a certain bewilderment in looking at things which only became more obscure the more precise they were. Out of this bewilderment, I thought, one could attempt to make a project: a house, for example.

One could attempt a project, or a novel, or a film, which stopped at this house, which could have a paved courtyard and then an entrance to another small courtyard separated by a gate from the garden, and beyond the garden, or in the garden, other houses and a hospital. And the house would have two stories, with intermediate landings. Or it could be one story and be situated in the garden with brick factories behind it. Certainly this indifference to form can be identified with a kind of malaise resulting from the condition.

I felt that the disorder, if limited and somehow honest, might best correspond to our state of mind.

But I detested the arbitrary disorder that is indifferent to order, a kind of moral obtuseness, complacent well-being, forgetfulness.

To what, then, could I have aspired in my craft?

Certainly to small things, having seen that the possibility of great ones was historically precluded.

Perhaps the observation of things has remained my most important formal education; for observation later becomes transformed into memory. Now I seem to see all the things I have observed arranged like tools in a neat row; they are aligned as in a botanical chart, or a catalogue, or a dictionary. But this catalogue, lying somewhere between imagination and memory, is not neutral; it always reappears in several objects and constitutes their deformation and, in some way, their evolution.

I believe that it may be difficult for the critic to understand all this from outside.

The critic should write books like *Call me Ishmael,* a study of Melville by the American poet Charles Olson. Olson's extremely beautiful book understands and interprets not only Melville, but anyone who has set his mind to do something. Surely the case of Melville fascinates me because it has always explained the relation between observation and memory, even, if you will, the relation between analysis and memory.

In *Call me Ishmael,* Olson writes some very important things which I prefer to quote at length here, even though I would like to keep quotations to a minimum in this book:

"In the *Journal Up the Straits*, the story of Melville's return starts after Cape Finisterre is passed, off Cape Vincent. The entry for that day is a dumb show of what is to follow. The contraries of the man who now turns to the East for some resolution of them lie in these natural sentences, as outward as gestures:

Sunday, Nov. 23, 1856 — 'Sunday 23d. Passed within a third of a mile of Cape St. Vincent. Light house & monastery on bold cliff. Cross. Cave underneath light house. The whole Atlantic breaks here. Lovely afternoon. Great procession of ships bound for Crimea must have been descried from this point.'

"Melville had started a ghost. What he sees on the cliff is, quick, his, life: HEIGHT and CAVE, with the CROSS between. And his books are made up of these things: light house, monastery, Cross, cave, the Atlantic, an afternoon, the Crimea: truth, celibacy, Christ, the great dark, space of ocean, the senses, man's past."

The enumeration of observed things is identified with Melville's life and writing, except that he notes the things that he has always seen and always experienced.

Even the search for the unforeseen is united or reunited with some form of the real.

I could ask myself what "the real" signifies in architecture. For example, might it be a dimensional, functional, stylistic, or technological fact? I could certainly write a treatise based on such facts.

But instead I think of a certain lighthouse, of a memory and of a summer. How does one establish the dimensions of these things, and indeed, what dimensions do they have? In this summer of 1977 I was staying at the Osteria della Maddalena when I came upon an architectural definition in the course of a conversation that was otherwise not very memorable.

I have transcribed it: "There was a sheer drop of ten meters from the highest point of the room." I do not know the context that this sentence refers to, but I find that a new dimension was established: is it possible to live in rooms which drop off so suddenly and precipitously? Does the possibility exist of inventing such a project, a representation which lies beyond memory and experience?

It is useless for me to declare that I have tried in vain to draw this project or this room: I could do it if it were not for the fact that the drawing always stops at a void which cannot be represented.

For many reasons this void is both happiness and its absence.

I have already said that the project at Chieti was based on happiness and that, in general, after I had finished off the subject of death in the project at Modena, I pursued the formal representation of happiness.

Now it is clear to me that there is no moment of complete happiness which does not contain in itself a form of idiocy, of authentic or recovered stupidity, like the game in which two children look in one another's eyes and the one who laughs first loses.

24

But it turned out that happiness made me think of beaches, and I superimposed the Adriatic coast and Versilia, Normandy and Texas: these are places which of course I know only fragmentarily, yet I have always sought in them the counterpoint to the world of the lake, which perhaps does not exactly represent happiness.

The sea seemed to me a coalescence capable of constructing a mysterious, geometric form made up of every memory and expectation. Perhaps it was really a verse from Alcaeus that led me to architecture when I was in secondary school: "O seashell / daughter of stone and the whitening sea / you astonish the minds of children." The lines go approximately like this, and in them are contained the problem of form, of material, of imagination—that is, of astonishment. I have always thought that to reduce the origin of material to some positivistic meaning constituted a distortion of both the material and the form.

I became aware of this idea in the project at Chieti and in *The Cabins of Elba*, an often published drawing, which could justly be called famous.

The cabins represented a completed architecture, but they also existed very much in the present, aligned along the sand and the white streets on timeless, unchanging mornings.

I admit that in this sense they represent a particular aspect of form and happiness: youth.

Yet this aspect is not essential, although it is bound up with my love for summers spent by the sea.

Then again, perhaps in thinking of stupidity, of the green of the blinds, of the sun, I must go farther back, as far as the Hotel Sirena, situated on the highway below S., by the lake.

The Hotel Sirena is so fundamental to my architecture that someone may think of it as my invention, as one of my projects. I might add that because of its courtyard typology, it also embodies an aspect of my architectural analysis of building volumes.

In reality, though, it is not the typological aspect of the hotel which has influenced my work, but its color—certainly from the point of view of the marvelous. The Hotel Sirena was covered entirely with a kind of green stucco which was used around 1940 and which my grandparents had also used on their villa. The mixture of this acid, excessive green with the forms of the petit-bourgeois villa, a combination not lacking in Romantic subtleties, offered a version of surrealism that lay between fascism and idiocy. By this I mean that it possessed certain vulgarly aggressive elements which I still cannot tolerate today, even though they fascinate me. All things considered, there is no doubt that these elements, emerging out of the color green, are linked to the name Sirena.

At this point, without leaving the scientific confines of this text, I must admit that the principal association between the hotel and the green was represented by a girl who was named, in contrast, Rosanna or Rossana, and the sense of paint and contrasting colors was never disentangled in me: specifically the oppositions between the acid green and this rose rosanna, between the color of flesh and a slightly unusual flower, all of which were enclosed in the image of the Sirena.

Truly every architecture is also an architecture of the interior or, better, an architecture from the interior: the blinds that filter the sunlight or the line of the water, together with the color and form of the bodies that live, sleep, and love one another behind the blinds, constitute, from the interior, another facade. These bodies also have their own color and light, a reflected light, so to speak; this light has something of the weariness or physical exhaustion of the summer, a sort of dazzling white among wintry tones.

This idea reappeared in the drawing of the cabins as little innocent houses—as the innocence of undressing by repeating old and familiar movements, as wet clothing, a game or two, the acid warmth of the sea salt. In northern Portugal I have seen huge cabins that resemble houses of this type, the *palheiros* of Mira, which are made of the grayish-white wood of wrecks run aground with porch-like landings for boats. This wood of both boat and house has a gray skeletal color that everyone recognizes: it is like the color of ships' hulls abandoned by the sea on some beach for years or centuries. It conjures up those fantastic illustrations of pirates' skeletons surrounded by their treasures, by precious stones and emeralds that time cannot devour, images which suggest a tangle of untold stories.

The translation of all this into architecture can be found in certain Mannerist fragments, in Alberti's Tempio, in turn-of-the-century factories and markets, in the aedicules behind churches, and certainly in confessionals. Confessionals are like small houses within a larger architectural structure, and they suggest how the duomo or cathedral of an old city would look as a covered part of the city.

Markets, cathedrals, public buildings, display a complex history of the city and man. The sales booths inside markets and the confessionals and chapels inside cathedrals display this relation between the individual and the universal, translating it into a relation between the interior and exterior in architecture. Markets—especially those in France, in Barcelona, and also the Rialto in Venice—have always had a particular fascination for me, which is only partly linked to architecture. They are the things that I remember; the quantity of food on display never fails to impress me. Meat, fruit, fish, vegetables appear again and again at the various stalls or sections into which the market is divided, and the fish are particularly striking: they have such varied forms and appearances that they always seem fantastic in our world. Perhaps this architecture of the street and of things, of people and food, of the flux of life, is fixed forever in the *vuzzeria* at Palermo. But this always takes me back to other questions concerning Palermo and Seville, two very different cities.

When I think of markets, however, I always draw an analogy with the theater, and particularly the eighteenth-century theater, with its relation between stages as isolated places and the total space of the theater. In all of my architecture, I have always been fascinated by the theater, although I have done only three projects connected with it: the early project for the Teatro Paganini in the Piazza della Pilotta at Parma; the 1979 project for the Little Scientific Theater; and, more recently, the floating theater at Venice. This

12 "Two Lights, Cape Elizabeth,
Maine." Photograph by George Tice,
1971.

last project is particularly dear to me; it is one for which I have much affection.

I have always thought that the term *teatrino* was more complex than *teatro;* it refers not just to the size of the building but also to the private, specific, repetitive character of all that is fiction in the theater. Others have considered *teatrino* to be an ironic or diminutive word. Yet *teatrino,* as opposed to *teatro,* expresses not so much irony or childishness, even if these are closely linked to the theater, as a peculiar and almost secret quality which accentuates the theatrical. My terming of the 1979 project "scientific" has its source in a number of ideas: it is certainly a mixture of the anatomical theater in Padua and the *teatrino scientifico* in Mantua, an allusion both to the scientific function and to those puppet theaters where Goethe loved to spend time in his youth.

Teatrini were also simple, temporary structures. The temporary theater lasted as long as a midsummer love affair, as long as a feverish, uncertain season, and by autumn it was destroyed—just like Chekhov's play, so wisely framed between a dead gull and a gunshot. A *teatrino* was that place where events developed as part of life, but also where theatrical events, during summer, during the time of vacations, were signs of life.

These places or *teatrini* were fragments and opportunities, though perhaps they failed to anticipate other events; their dramas made no *progress.* In my *teatrino* an almost compulsory set of relations presides. I will leave out the mass of quotations, memories, obsessions, which people it; yet how can the designer of this project not cite the brief passage that Raymond Roussel wrote for his Theater of the Incomparables?
"On my right, in front of the trees, at a point in the middle of the row, stood a kind of red theater, like a gigantic Punch-and-Judy show, whose facade bore the words *The Incomparables Club* arranged in three lines of silver lettering, in a glittering surround of broad golden rays, spreading in every direction like those around a sun.
"On the stage at present a table and chair were to be seen, apparently intended for a lecturer. Several unframed portraits were pinned to the backcloth and underneath was an explanatory label worded thus: *Electors of Brandenburg.*"
Here is a true architectural project. The author also informs us that this theatrical vision occurs at four o'clock on June 25, and that although the sun has set, the heat is stifling because of the stormy weather. Furthermore, the theater is surrounded by an imposing capital city formed of innumerable huts.

The project is fixed in time and space: it is four o'clock inside an imposing capital. This imposing quality is offered by the huts, which are simple but innumerable.

There is also a clock on the front of this small theater, but it does not keep time. It has stopped at five o'clock; this hour may be earlier than four or it may even be the mythical hour of Ignacio Sanchez Mejias: when it is five o'clock in Seville during summer vacation, the clock of the arena ceases to tick away the time.

For certainly the time of the theater does not coincide with time measured by clocks, nor are emotions bound to chronological time; they are repeated on stage every evening with impressive punctuality and exactitude.

But the action is never extraneous to the ambience of the theater or *teatrino,* and all this is summed up in the little wooden tables, a stage, the sudden and unexpected lights, people. Herein lies the spell cast by the theater.

In recent projects, I have pursued these limitless analogies: the hut-like buildings for student housing at Chieti, the drawings of the cabins of Elba, the palm trees and the houses at Seville were all pieces of a system which were assembled inside the Little Scientific Theater. It became a laboratory where the result of the most precise experiment was always unforeseen. Yet nothing can yield more unforeseen results than a repetitive mechanism. And no mechanisms seem more repetitive in their typological aspects than the house, public buildings, the theater.

Of course, in seeking to comprehend the entire city, the architect passed through other theaters, other scales, and he found stone constructions which followed the topography of the land, comprising a new geography.

But later all this was lost.

Yet perhaps the greatest attempt at recovery was the invention of the theater as a specific place, from ancient Rome onward: the boards of the stage, the scenery that no longer seeks to imitate anything, the seats, the boxes, the dizzying quality of the fiction, actions and characters who in their continuous repetition, are nearly detached from intelligence and from the body—this entire world presents itself with the magic of the theater at the orchestra's first notes.

These first notes are always an initiation, and they possess all the magic of one. I realized as much while looking at empty theaters as if they were buildings abandoned forever, even though this abandonment in reality is often briefer than the length of a day. Still, this brief abandonment is so burdened with memory that it creates the theater.

Creating the theater: the historical examples I encountered, all in the Po valley, are for me confounded with each other and superimposed like the music of the lyric opera in village festivals—Parma, Padua, Pavia, Piacenza, Reggio, and even Venice, Milan, and all the Po capitals where the theater shines its lights into the persistent fog. This is the same fog that penetrates the Galleria in Milan, which I spoke of earlier, like some effect produced by a theatrical machine. And in the midst of the fog, like an individual dwelling, stands the theater. Certainly, the theater, as a way of life, is a dwelling. And I found it again, in its essential form, in other, distant dwellings. For example, in the little cities of inland Brazil, the theater is distinguished by nothing more than the clear articulation of the tympanum, by the unique and subtle devices of the facade. I also found this essential form inside the cathedrals where the *retablo* appears like a fixed scene around which stages are arranged or carved out.

I linger in these places, trying to grasp the possibilities of the architecture, measuring the spaces, noting the placement of the atrium, the stairs, the stages, which become modified in the various expansions or compressions of

30

*14 Houses in Mira, northern
Portugal, 1976.*

the distances between the parts. Scarcely do we experience a sense of largeness than we realize the deception of the proportions, just as we comprehend that the different elements in the work are woven strangely together, illuminating one another. Perhaps the magic of the theater especially resides in this mixture of suggestion and reality.

Hence the invention of the Little Scientific Theater, like any theatrical project, is an imitation; and like every good project, it is concerned only with being a tool, an instrument, a useful space where a definitive action can occur. The theater is thus inseparable from its stage sets, its models, the experience of every combination; and the stage is reduced to the artisan's or scientist's work-table. It is experimental as science is experimental, but it casts its peculiar spell on every experiment. Inside the theater nothing can be accidental, yet nothing can be permanently resolved either.

I think of two plays which could forever be alternated with one another: the first is entitled *The Unreconciled*, the second, *The Reunited*. People, events, things, fragments, architecture always have something which precedes or follows them and they continuously intersect one another, as in the puppet theaters of Bergamo which I remember from my childhood on the lake: the punctually repeated *Betrothed* showed us events which always developed according to some impossibility, and characters who, like Hamlet, had to resolve a dimly understood, predetermined fate. But every evening on that branch of the lake, the same curtain, framed by its own lights and architecture, indicated one possibility.

This was the fiction of the theater—and also its science and its magic.

The theater, in which the architecture serves as a possible background, a setting, a building that can be calculated and transformed into the measurements and concrete materials of an often elusive feeling, has been one of my passions, even if I do not always like to admit it.

For I have always preferred the bricklayers, engineers, and builders who created one form, who constructed that which rendered one definite action possible. Yet the theater, and perhaps only the theater, possesses the unique magical ability to transform every situation.

I ask myself how the seasons enter into architecture. I pause at the Milanese Galleria in the winter when the fog has entered it; or in Brazil I stop to look at the landscape, at the human bodies which consume every private space, or at abandoned villas by the lake.

I pause at situations that might very well be my own architecture, where the configuration of time and place, which seems so important, dissolves into habitual gestures and paths.

This sensibility presided over a project which has often been described in different ways and which I have called *Project for a Villa with Interior.* *Forgetting Architecture* is perhaps a much more appropriate title. I seem to have gradually abandoned this project, even though I often speak of it, and it turns up among my papers in unfinished drawings and plans or in postcards and photographs already yellowed by time. There were materials that I wanted to construct it with—perhaps the film that I wanted to make, but that increasingly confounded people, light, and things. At first, moreover, this interior was nothing more than some furnishings, but later it also became people, the presence of bodies. At times I like to think that I have forever lost all trace of this project, if it were not for the fact that it re-presents itself on various occasions.

I have mentioned that the villa, whether large or small, has nothing to do with the small house; this is something that the old masters have explained to us. After the Romans, the *locus* or place of the villa was for all time defined by Palladio in his writings and his built works: the desanctification of the form of the religious temple and the choice of location (high grounds, watercourses, gardens, lakes) are his greatest inventions. Historically, this reduction permitted the development of the romantic and petit-bourgeois villa, and even palaces, which were the transformation of garden pavilions into villas: such is the secret of this building type. One need only think of Schinkel's villa-pavilion in the park at Charlottenburg.

In the wake of these ideas, the architecture of the villa was destined to dissolve and nearly disappear, hardly leaving a trace of its increasingly fantastic typologies. The Palladian idea of space took the villa out of its context; this space, with which we are so familiar, can be found both along the Rio Paraná and on Lake Como, in New England and on the Mediterranean—in short, anywhere one wishes. Much of the beauty of Raymond Chandler's stories is based on his intimate knowledge of the villa, so much so that while he makes this architecture the element which defines an event's taking place in California, with slight changes it could indicate another setting as well. One always recognizes the gate, the hydrangeas, the tire tracks on the gravel, a table which is about to be set, certain greetings and rather remote words. Chekhov's interiors also more closely resemble those of villas than country houses, and they are always extremely sensitive to the seasons. The architecture remains in the small details, as if forever awaiting the sound of the shooting of the "gull," the light on the stair, the boat which crosses the lake as in a glass dome.

My project for the villa is perhaps an attempt to find again this architecture which filters that distinctive light, that evening coolness, those shadows of a summer afternoon. *Azul de atardecer.*

In the project there is a long, narrow corridor sealed off at either end by a glass door: the first opens onto a narrow street; the second, onto the lake from where the blue of the water and the sky enters the villa. Of course, whether a corridor or a room, it is inevitably a place in which someone will say sooner or later, "Must we talk about all this?" or "See how things have changed!" and other things that seem to be taken from some screenplay or drama. The long afternoons and the children's shouts and the time spent with the family also are inevitable, because the architect had foreseen that the continuity of the house depended on its *corridor*—and not just in terms of its plan. When I sketch the line of a corridor, I see in it this aspect of path, and perhaps because of this, the project did not go any farther. The corridor was a strip of space that seemed surrounded and gripped by private acts, unforseeable occasions, love affairs, repentances.

And especially by images which do not leave their imprint on film but which accumulate in things. For this reason, the interior is important: one must always imagine the effect produced by a person who leaves a room unexpectedly. One asks oneself whether there are adjoining rooms and similar questions, which ultimately mingle with considerations about protection against dampness, water levels, roofs, and finally, the soundness of the construction.

It turns out that this idea of the interior, like the green of the garden, is stronger than the building itself. You can already read the project in existing houses, select it from a repertory which you can easily procure, pursue it in the variants of its production, in the actor's cues, in the atmosphere of the theater, and always be surprised by Hamlet's uncertainties, never knowing whether he is truly a good prince, as everything conspires to make us believe.

Perhaps a design is merely the space where the analogies in their identification with things once again arrive at silence.

The relationships are a circle that is never closed; only a fool would think of adding the missing part or changing the meaning of the circle. Not in purism but in the unlimited *contaminatio* of things, of correspondences, does silence return. The drawing can be suggestive, for as it limits it also amplifies memory, objects, events.

A design pursues this fabric of connections, memories, images, yet knowing that in the end it will have to be definitive about this or that solution; on the other hand, the original, whether in its true or presumed state, will be an obscure object which is identified with its copy.

Even technique seems to stop at a threshold where its discipline dissolves.

Photographs, reliefs, drawings, the plot of a drama, the screenplay of a film.

Perhaps a portrait.

Here one can terminate the inventory of projects or, if one wishes, begin an exhaustive search for things, a search which is also a recollection, but which is above all the destructive aspect of the experience that proceeds unforeseen, giving and taking away significance from each project, event, thing, or person.

The idea of the villa grew in this way and was transformed through the multiplication of rooms and the rigid extension of the straight corridor, becoming a hospital, convent, barracks, the site of an incommunicable yet ever-present collective life. I have always thought that in every action there has to be something coercive, and this idea applies not only to relationships between people and things but also to the imagination. It is difficult to think without some obsession; it is impossible to create something imaginative with-

16 A villa at Lake Maggiore.

out a foundation that is rigorous, incontrovertible and, in fact, repetitive. This is the meaning of many of my projects, as well as of my interest in the market square, the theater, the house.

Thus I now understand the mysterious observation I had gleaned in the Osteria della Maddalena: that is, I understand that in every room there is a sheer drop, a plunge into space, but it would be as foolish to try to construct that precipitous place as it would be to construct intimacy, happiness, or ruin. Only lately have I learned how to understand Victorian interiors, dim lights, faded curtains, the horror of empty spaces which must be filled completely and always covered and veiled. In *Project for a Villa with Interior* I asked myself these things, and perhaps because of my questions, I did not arrive at any logic which would complete the design. I could not even refer to that vulgar image of the Hotel Sirena, because at this point the hotel was a monument where I participated in a repetitive and necessary liturgy for its own sake.

Today if I were to talk about architecture, I would say that it is a ritual rather than a creative process. I say this fully understanding the bitterness and the comfort of the ritual.

Rituals give us the comfort of continuity, of repetition, compelling us to an oblique forgetfulness, allowing us to live with every change which, because of its inability to evolve, constitutes a destruction.

This may explain many of my drawings and projects. In 1966 the project for the housing block in San Rocco proposed an absolute rationality; it was the Roman grid imposed on a piece of Lombardy. It could have been extended to infinity: there was something perfect about this project, yet almost lifeless, detached. Then I realized that the two parts of the grid should be offset, but only slightly. The mirror remained in its frame, yet it was broken in a way that could be described not as a desire for asymmetry, but rather as an accident which slightly altered the reflection of the face. Or if the reflection was not altered, certainly it was slightly disjointed.

This expressed my horror and critique of *limitatio*. It reminded me of the farmers in the Veneto who, as a result of their centuries-old poverty, broke down the Roman measurement of the fields, building on both the *cardo* and the *decumanus*. This has always impressed me because it shows how the street, the element of public order, escaped being subjected to private ownership as the fields were, and therefore could not be claimed by a state in ruins or by an abstract empire. Or else my critique of *limitatio* was like the result of a movement of the earth, a geological settling which changed the axes of building. I always liked the settling of the Pantheon described in the books on statics; the unforeseen crack, the visible but contained collapse, gave immense strength to the architecture because its beauty could not have been anticipated.

The work of Alessandro Antonelli was certainly among my early enthusiasms for architecture. I have always admired his obsession and passion for vertical construction. Many of his buildings collapsed, while some continue to stand with an equilibrium that is practically ineffable. Antonelli carried to the extreme the brick dome, a system of traditional construction which inevitably had to be abandoned. He was opposed to breaking the ancient rules; he felt as if they had no equal in modern techniques because of their elemental nature. This passion for technique is very important for my projects and my interest in architecture. I believe that my building in the Gallaratese quarter of Milan may be significant, above all, because of the simplicity of its construction, which allows it to be repeated. For the same reason, I have always loved the work of Gaudì, even if it seems that this interest may be an homage to my friend Salvador Tarragò. Actually, I did learn about Gaudì's greatness from Salvador, yet the structural rules became my own: the practice of taking the possibilities of engineering to absurd lengths, the forest of columns in Güell Park where the supporting structures bend according to structural or surreal laws, the extraordinary *mezcla* or mixture of engineering and imagination, autobiography and religion, which Salvador described to me in Catalan. Of course, what made Gaudì's work possible was statics, the same principles which figured in the construction of the Colossus of Rhodes, the Empire State Building, the San Carlone, the Mole Antonelliana, the aqueduct at Córdoba, the rockets in Houston, the Pyramids, the twin towers of the World Trade Center, and other things which I cannot describe, like the wells at Orvieto.

Perhaps I took an interest in architecture because of the mythical legends about the Great Wall of China or the tombs at Mycenae. I knew that all this had ended, or that perhaps it had never really occurred. Yet these constructions made by human labor impressed me, like the wax figure of the man I saw repeatedly in the Sacri Monti, in the caves of Palermo, and hanging in the churches of Brazil.

I understand that this is the aim of all techniques: the identification of the object with the imagination of it. But the aim is also to bring the imagination back to its base, to its foundation, to the earth and to the flesh.

I am disgusted by anyone who speaks of art as "liberation." Such a comment belongs to superficial criticism and, ultimately, to a superficial conception of art. As in the statues of the Sacri Monti of S., which I passed almost every day, what I admired was not their art; rather I pursued the relentlessness, the story, the repetition, and was content that in some way, even if it were painful, virtue would triumph in the end. It is like seeing the same film or play many times and thus being free from the desire to know the end. To experience this effect I often go to the cinema when the film is half over or just ending; in this way one meets the characters in their conclusive moments, and then one can rediscover the action that happened earlier or imagine an alternative.

I must make a few more comments about the cemetery at Modena, the first version of which dates back to a competition held in 1971. Around that time I began to write the first notes for this text, which I collected in those small blue books intended for exercises and notes that are to be found only in Switzerland. They are a beautiful shade of blue, and I call them "the blue notebooks."

In the project for the cemetery at Modena, as I have said, I sought to resolve the youthful problem of death through representation. I know very well that this may not be the best way to begin an explanation of a project, nor is the skeletal mediation or meditation on bones which I have already mentioned.

38

Beyond these things, though, there still clearly existed in this project a mediation between the object and its representation, a mediation which somehow vanished from subsequent projects. The central concept of the cemetery was perhaps my realization that the things, objects, buildings of the dead are not different from those of the living. I have referred to the Roman tomb of the baker, an abandoned factory, an empty house; I also saw death in the sense of "no one lives here anymore" and hence as regret, since we do not know what our relations with this person were, and yet we still search for him in some way.

My project subsequently became identified with the distance or path required to get to its site, ultimately its construction site. Such relationships between distances and the several places where I have built are unique. They are like an obligatory diversion or a compulsory relationship; they always have the precise quality that only a purpose can confer on a journey. Perhaps I have never taken a journey as a true tourist, even though my purposes for traveling were many and not just linked to work.

Yet here I am referring simply to the landscape, to the places between Modena and Parma which I have rediscovered with each visit and continue to rediscover, and the same could certainly be said of many other places. This bond to places and its opposite are very important, even though I do not succeed in expressing it clearly.

My frequent visits to this landscape have never changed much for me, nor have they changed my original preferences at all.

Whenever I followed the progress of my few realized projects, I liked the errors made on the construction site, the little deformations, the changes which became remedial in some unexpected way. Indeed, they amazed me because they began to seem the life of the structure. As a matter of fact, I believe that any original order is open to practical changes, and that it allows for all the failures of human weakness. Because of this belief, my commitment has always been fundamentally different from that of my contemporaries and professors; thus, at the Politecnico in Milan, I believe that I was one of the worst students, although today I think that the criticisms addressed to me then are among the best compliments I have ever received. Professor Sabbioni, whom I particularly admired, discouraged me from making architecture, saying that my drawings looked like those of a bricklayer or a rural contractor who threw a stone to indicate approximately where a window was to be placed. This observation, which made my friends laugh, filled me with joy, and today I try to recover that felicity of drawing which was confused with inexperience and stupidity, and which has subsequently characterized my work. In other words, a great part of the meaning and evolution of time escaped me and still does so today, as if time were a material which I observe only from the outside. The lack of evolution in my work has been the source of some misunderstanding, but it also brings me joy.

If this is my current position, and if a position can somehow be continuous, I must still try to give an order to my work, to pursue the chronology of this scientific autobiography. As I have said, I was not interested principally in architecture: I think it is significant that my first published article was entitled

"*La coscienza di poter 'dirigere la natura'* [The Awareness of the Power to Control Nature]." It is a text of 1954, and I was twenty-three years old at the time. On the other hand, one of the most important architectural studies I have written dates back to this period. This second essay was published in 1956, but written about a year before. It is entitled "The Concept of Tradition in Neoclassical Milanese Architecture."

I mention these two texts since they concern the history of an epoch, specifically the social history.

When I was around twenty years old, I was invited to the Soviet Union. This was a particularly happy time for me, and as a result of it my youth became associated with an experience which was then unique. I loved everything about Russia: socialist realism as well as the old cities, the people and the landscape. My interest in socialist realism helped me rid myself of the entire petit-bourgeois culture of modern architecture: I preferred the alternative of the broad streets of Moscow, the pleasant and provocative architecture of the subway, and the university on Lenin's hills. I saw emotion mixing with a desire to construct a new world. Many people now ask me what that period meant to me, and I believe I have to say, above all, that I became conscious of the possibility that architecture could be unified with popular pride, like the pride of the students of Moscow and the farmers by the Don, who showed me schools and houses. I have never returned to the Soviet Union, but I am proud that I have always defended the great architecture of the Stalinist period, which could have been transformed into an important alternative for modern architecture but was abandoned for no clear reason. A friend recently sent me a postcard from Moscow which reproduces the university in the greenish-blue light of the meadow and the sky, and I noted with joy how these buildings are authentic monuments that also have the capacity to be faithful to that holiday atmosphere which is displayed on every tourist postcard. My defense of Soviet architecture has always involved me in polemics, but I have never abandoned it. I am also aware that my obstinacy may have what I would call a private or autobiographical character. One morning, after being released from a brief stay at a hospital in Odessa, I was walking along the sea and I had the precise perception of a memory, or rather I was positively reliving this moment as a memory. I rediscovered this same experience in Vassily Sushkin's film *A Man's Life*, which I also associate with Alexander Dovzhenko's *Michurin*, the film which became the basis of my essay on "The Awareness of the Power to Control Nature." This seems to me a silly title, but it is like a program, and like every program, it remains independent of its shortcomings.

In speaking of places, the Russia of my early youth and the others I later visited, I see how a scientific investigation of one's work becomes almost a geography of one's education. And perhaps if I had developed this book according to a different scheme, I could have called it *The Geography of My Projects*.

Certainly every place is unique to the extent that it possesses limitless affinities or analogies with other places; even the concept of identity, and hence
40

that of difference, is relative.

Each place is remembered to the extent that it becomes a place of affection, or that we identify with it. I think of Antonioni's film *Professione: Reporter (The Passenger)* and of a place particularly dear to me on the island of Elba to which we gave the same name, although there is no apparent resemblance between the place and the film apart from the light and the sun. Yet the association is also appropriate because this place was connected with a loss of identity, as was Antonioni's film. This place was one of my projects.

It has always been my intention to write about architectural projects, narratives, films, and paintings in a way that is more and more dissociated from their respective techniques, since in this way the creative process would be more closely identified with the thing described and would simultaneously be a projection of reality. I thought of selecting a few projects and examining them from many points of view, but this is not easily done when there is a chronological order. For example, I realize that in discussing Antonioni's film I was alluding to the drawing *The Cabins of Elba*, but this later became the project for student housing at Chieti, while in other drawings I have called it *Impressions d'Afrique* (and not only as an homage to Raymond Roussel). Thus I believe that a project may be a conclusion to a chain of associations, or else may actually be forgotten and left to other people or situations.

This kind of forgetting is also associated with a loss of our own identity and that of the things we observe; every change occurs within a moment of obsession. The difference between the long urban building I had designed for the Gallaratese quarter in Milan about ten years earlier and these small houses of Elba seems to me to elucidate my one idea about the city and the places where we live: they should be seen as part of the reality of human life. They are like copies of different observations and times: my youthful observation of long workers' scaffolds, of courtyards full of voices and meetings which I spied on with a sort of fear in my bourgeois childhood, had the same fascination as the cabins or, better, as the small houses which came to mind in other situations and places—like the monks' houses at the Certosa in Pavia or those endless American suburbs.

The small house is, as I said, fundamentally different from the villa. Like the loggia and the courtyard, it makes for a village, a familiarity, a bond which even in the best houses becomes an enforced feeling. At times it seems to me that there is not much difference between a small house at the center of an African village, one in an Alpine village, and one secluded in the vast expanse of America. There exists an entire technical terminology to describe this so-called small house. Yet I realized this for the first time in my drawings for *The Cabins of Elba*, which date back, I believe, to 1973. I called them cabins because not only are they actually given this term in practice and in conversation, but also because they seem to me a minimal dimension of life, like an impression of the summer. For this reason in other drawings I later called them *Impressions d'Afrique*, here also with reference to the world of Roussel, who tells us at the beginning that "the theater was surrounded by an imposing capital city formed of innumerable huts." These innumerable huts or cabins surrounding the mass of the theater gave me a vision of a type of city and building. In the 1976 project at Chieti, I associated this vision with student housing, which we generally think of as a large or small residential structure (even on American campuses), just as I had envisioned it myself in my Trieste project of 1977. Now I envisioned a village, in which an unfinished public building with huge girders stood atop massive brick walls. A Mediterranean-African appearance was created by these cabins as well as by the large palms which I had thought about for years and which turn up everywhere in my observation, not only in the broad streets of Seville (where the small houses similarly constitute a city which one identifies with vacation and hence summer), but also aligned along the lake in front of the houses, where I have always found them to be like a signal, a symbol, the very memory of a house.

Thus the small house, hut, cabin conformed to, and was deformed by, the place and the people, and nothing could replace it or take away this private, almost personal character of identification with the body, with undressing and getting dressed again. But this relation with the body also recurred with a remote and apparently opposite meaning in the huts of the Alps, in the stories of farmers gathered in stables, and finally in the small, analogous construction of the confessional. Confessionals stand as simple structures within the large buildings that generally stand out from a village; they are small, well-constructed houses where one speaks of secret things, where one speaks of the body with the very pleasure and uneasiness of the summer cabins. They are provided with a roof, windows, decorations; often the name of the priest is written on the door as if he were the owner of the house. And this small house is often transformed into a cemetery. For this reason, San Carlo Borromeo, although busy with great architectural and social projects, tried to make the confessional-house more human by prohibiting the deposit of bones in it, even though this was customarily done for devotional and spiritual purposes; and in order to vanquish this ancient ritual, he himself scoured his beloved Valsolda with the aid of a few people, emptying out even the most remote confessionals. Thus, in the small house even more than in the church, the Counter-Reformation tried to dissolve the strong original unity between body and soul. Equally persistent and laborious was the intervention of the Jesuits in the small houses which they constructed for the Indians: they rearranged walls, divisions, separations, so that these hut-like houses would immediately become places where some separation between body and soul occurred.

With *The Cabins of Elba*, I wanted to reduce the house to the values it has in the seasons. The small house is not merely a reduction of the villa in scale; it is the antithesis of the villa. The villa presupposes both infinite interiors like labyrinths and gardens, however small they may actually be, and a *locus*. The small house, on the other hand, seems to be *without* place, because the *locus* is inside, or is identified with whoever lives in the house for a time—a stay which we know may be brief but which we cannot calculate.

The cabin, as I see it, always has four walls and a tympanum; the tympanum is more than functional, since it also suggests a banner and its color. The colored stripes are an integral and determining part, perhaps the most obviously architectonic part of the structure. This part, above all, makes us aware that there has to be some event in the interior, and that somehow in the acting out of the event a performance will take place. How, then, can one separate the cabin from another of its meanings—the theater? My Little Scientific Theater of 1979 developed from these cabin drawings, and it was precisely its function which impelled me to call it "scientific," just as I call my autobiography of these projects scientific, hoping that my analyses will bring about some kind of salvation, not through me or my craft, but through the progress which comes out of all analyses.

Thus I can now better place the small house in real and fantastic landscapes. The connotations of the cabins of Elba and the Little Scientific Theater contain in themselves so much that is private and autobiographical that they permit me to pursue what would otherwise remain fixated within a self-consuming desire for the past. As a result I can regard "my cabins" like any other observer, since they are not transfixed in a single summer, and they simultaneously become a wardrobe, dressing room, house, theater, small cemetery.

Yet having retraced this path, I still find myself returning to the magnificent, changeable landscape which stretches along the Adriatic in every season, just as I observed it when I was teaching at Pescara around 1966. We saw the land rise with the approach of the summer and subside with its decline—a season much longer than that of Seville, with its dramatic city of the summer holidays, a time of vacation, meetings, affairs, perhaps even tedium, which recurs year after year. And when the vast beaches of the Adriatic were empty in winter, they were still the mobile terrain of a temporary city which the seaside promenade separates from the other, permanent city. Yet the temporary city of Seville always remains for me the city of encounters and intersections, like the breakwater, like everything that lies between land and water, between land and sky.

Thus in the intersections between land and sky, forest and sky, lies one of my favorite projects, the house at Borgo Ticino, which I began to design in 1973. The first and clearest drawing was nothing more than a forest with houses built on piers, and it was entitled *On the Street of Varallo Piombia* and dated. Yet in the technique of this drawing, the idea or its representation still has not filtered through; indeed, it looks like the work of someone who was merely reporting on a day, a place, a street. Yet if the falsification of the facts, the insubstantiality of the encounters, the very point of the thing disappears in the subsequent project, the small, elevated house remains. Its balconies have become piers—the floating type—recalling those on the Ticino or on the Hudson or any river.

These are all elements of an architectural treatise.

To forget architecture, or any proposition, was the objective of my unchanging choice of a typology of pictorial and graphic construction in which the graphics became confused with handwriting, as in certain highly developed forms of graphic obsession where the marks may be seen as either drawing or writing. I recently saw a letter which Paul Hofer sent me, and his handwriting, as relentlessly vertical and apparently clear as the characters in Gothic missals, moved me: the writing itself became a drawing, as in the work of his countryman Paul Klee. Hofer's writing reminded me of his magnificent lectures at the Federal Polytechnical Institute in Zurich, where his perfect German, which I followed with difficulty, was often combined with French according to the custom of the Bernese bourgeoisie. His letter was accompanied by a very beautiful drawing of my Gallaratese building in Milan which he had made during a visit to that city with his students. Yet for me the letter and the drawing became superimposed on images of Zurich, Bern, Fribourg, Colmar. These cities were my favorites during the years I taught at Zurich, and everything I am now writing goes back to a little notebook which I entitled the *Colmar Notebook*. Now this project for Colmar was similar to the one for Solothurn which I was supposed to do with Paul Hofer. In fact it was never done, but it has penetrated my drawings like a secret spring. Little by little the towers of Solothurn were superimposed on Filarete's column, while the rigid metal banner creaks against the cold white sky in every drawing.

"To creak" is the translation of the German *klirren*, which has always struck me in Hölderlin's poem "Halfte des Lebens." The very title of the poem seems to me a condition of suspension. The little iron banners which Hölderlin never drew himself subsequently invaded my drawings, and I am unable to answer any further the persistent questions I am asked about them except to say that I have translated the last lines of Hölderlin's poem into my architecture: "*Die Maurern stehn / Sprachlos und kalt, im Winde / Klirren die Fahnen* [The walls stand / mute and cold, in the wind / the banners creak]." I concluded one of my lectures at Zurich with this quotation, which I applied to my projects: "*Meine Architektur steht sprachlos und kalt* [My architecture stands mute and cold]."

This *sprachlos* is more than mute though; in fact, I think of an absence of words rather than a muteness. The difficulty of the word often creates an inexhaustible verbal continuity, as with certain expressions of Hamlet or Mercutio. "Thou talk'st of nothing" is a way of saying nothing and everything—something similar to that graphic obsession I spoke of just before. I recognize this in many of my drawings, in a type of drawing where the line is no longer a line, but writing.

Hence this form of writing which lies midway between drawing and handwriting fascinated me for a long while, even if at the same time it made me peculiarly uneasy. There are some written drawings, such as those of Giacometti and the sixteenth-century Mannerists, which especially fascinated me. Similarly the statements of Adolf Loos, with their almost Biblical character, excited me because they could not be further developed, because they constituted an a-historical logic of architecture.

Loos made this great architectural discovery by identifying himself with the object through observation and description—without changing, without yielding, and finally, without creative passion, or rather with his sense of being frozen in time. But it is difficult and often amateurish to speak directly of one's own emotions. While I admit that there is sometimes a squalid beauty in tavern talk, perhaps only Shakespeare knew how to reproduce the tension inherent in this disparity between subject and expression.

Loos's kind of frozen description also appears in the great Renaissance theorists, in the categories of Alberti, in Dürer's letters; but the practice, craft, and technique they had followed vanished, because from the beginning it was not important enough to transmit or translate.

Into what?

As in the old oratorio transcribed for me by P., four figures alternated: Time,

Beauty, Disillusionment, Pleasure. The outcome was predetermined, but it was not less interesting because of this. Obviously Time won, but the other characters' parts became exciting because they were simple functions of Time. I detested Disillusionment and loved Pleasure for its discretion: as always it was the rhetorical figure of Pleasure that was forced to withdraw, but Pleasure was also the best part of everyday life; it promised small joys. It was a reduction of life and of the theater that was somehow possible.

In architecture every window is the window both of the artist and of anybody at all, the window children write about in letters: "Tell me what you see from your window." In reality, a window is an aperture like any other, which perhaps opens out on a simple native village; or it is simply any opening from which one can lean out. Moreover, the window, like the coffin, presents an incredible history. Of course, from the point of view of construction, the window and the coffin resemble one another; and the window and coffin, like the palace, like everything else, anticipate events which have already happened, somewhere, here or some other place.

Perhaps signs can be changed when a story is retold, but the tangible signs with which a story is conveyed are what we can still call a history or a design. Apart from his identification with the object, this idea is Adolf Loos's observation or discovery in the face of the grave. Early in 1979 I saw the first wing of the cemetery at Modena being filled with the dead, and these corpses with their yellowish-white photographs, their names, the plastic flowers offered out of family and public sympathy, gave the place its unique significance. But then after many polemics it went back to being the great house of the dead where the architecture was a scarcely perceptible background for the specialist. In order to be significant, architecture must be forgotten, or must present only an image for reverence which subsequently becomes confounded with memories.

Likewise, every theater is subsumed by Roussel's description, which shatters every image of the theater by referring to it as something that has always existed, that arises in one place as in any other, and whose major distinction is its inscription "THEATER." This inscription is its emblem and final seal, and whatever the theater, the label simply falls into place. A similar thing occurs in children's drawings, where the inscription "THEATER," "CITY HALL," "HOUSE," "SCHOOL," serves to define and refer to the actual edifice that the child is unable to draw. Architecture is a reference in everyone's experience. But it should only be evident insofar as it serves imagination or action: even the dreary functionalists partially understood this.

There were rooms, hotels, boardinghouses, the train station in the village where someone held the slightly dilapidated suitcase, the train that was so late that there was no longer anything to talk about, and the tedium which increased beneath passion and mistrust. Between France and Germany someone said "Siegfried" as in a drama. But the most mysterious boundary was perhaps that of the beginning; and the long sheds by the lake which did not recall architecture or what we call atmosphere, which forgot about design, and having forgotten it, could not be clearly recounted. This oblivion of design

45

was the idea that Renaissance theorists tried to express—more in images than in general rules—and that the great positivists, like Viollet-le-Duc, sought in history, conducting a mad search for the perfect function through the classification of every part.

Yet when I was writing *The Architecture of the City*, I must say I felt a profound admiration for Viollet-le-Duc: what he did was like a game, a challenge to history, a total trust in a sign that was devoid of drama—it was not unlike Ludwig of Bavaria's castles. Modern architecture has treated all these things in an insane way, searching for some unknown purity: yet this was our tradition. In reality, everything became so reduced that it could no longer be touched. I do not wish to play the critic, but I believe that after Schinkel's house at Charlottenburg, architecture became a matter of mere formal cleverness bound up with production: if there remain any great architects associated with a people or country, they are Gaudì and Antonelli and many engineers whose names are unknown to us.

I have realized all this since my first years at the Politecnico. I certainly appreciated Sigfried Giedion's book, particularly because it was biased. It was based, above all, on his enthusiasm for Le Corbusier, about whom I myself have always suspended judgment. During the fifties, it was not possible for an intelligent young man to be enthusiastic about the great books of nineteenth-century architecture. I would rather not discuss this point here, since it would lead me too far afield. Nonetheless, it is significant to note that during this period the best young people devoted themselves to politics, film, and literature. All things considered, Giulio Argan's book on Gropius was a beautiful romance, but it was not concerned with facts. My favorite book was certainly that of Loos, which I read and studied on the recommendation of a man whom I should also call my mentor, Ernesto N. Rogers. I read Loos for the first time around 1959 in the beautiful first edition published by Brenner Verlag and given to me by Rogers. Perhaps this architect alone revealed the connection to the great questions: the Austrian and German tradition of Fischer von Erlach and Schinkel, local culture, handicrafts, history, and especially theater and poetry. Without doubt I owe to this reading of Loos the profound contempt I have always felt for industrial design and for the confounding of form and function. Through Loos I discovered Kraus, Schoenberg, Wittgenstein, and above all, Trakl, but also the great architecture of ancient Rome and an America which I would come to understand only much later. I read about all these subjects and artists perhaps in an ingenuous way, but this may have been the only way to do such reading. It has long gained me the reputation of being a Germanophile, if I may say so, and has led critics to relate all my work to the world of Central Europe. Of course, as my students and friends in Zurich and Germany know very well, my knowledge of the German language has always been inadequate, to say the least, but I am certain, as I believe I have already written in these pages, that a valuable discussion with my friend Heinrich Helfenstein on my translation of Hölderlin proved more salutary for my architecture than all the bad books and lectures of my professors at the Politecnico in Milan.

Before concluding these comments on several architectural texts, which have been, so to speak, fundamental for me, I must mention my translation of Etienne-Louis Boullée and my introduction to this work. I have been told, and I consider it a compliment, that this translation is not very faithful to the original, or that it is simply an invention. I admit that it is certainly a collaboration. This is partly due to the fact that Boullée's French is not easy to translate, and besides, I found in him a sympathetic consciousness whose like I have not found since. The book was published in 1967, and when I began it I was nearly thirty, so it cannot be considered a work of my youth. I believe that it was done at San Michele in a house by the sea. At times I think about how certain works accompany particular periods in one's life and how I identified myself in this situation with an old French academic like Boullée, but I recall being struck by Baudelaire's assertion that *correspondances* exist.

In the introductory essay to the Boullée translation I speak of conventional rationalism and exalted rationalism, but did I perhaps fail to notice that life itself was an exalted rationalism? Boullée thinks about a library and the library is its volumes: it is their weight that determines it, and not just in the sense of statics. The library is realized in a space which Boullée, like a visionary, traverses as if it were that of *The School of Athens*, for such is the space of these men through whom he walks. And what could be changed? What could be changed after his enormous discovery of light and shadow? Boullée explicitly asserts that he has discovered the architecture of shadows, and hence the architecture of light. With this insight he taught me how light and shadow are nothing but the other faces of chronological time, the fusion of that atmospheric and chronological *tempo* which displays and then consumes architecture, and presents an image of it that is brief yet simultaneously extended.

Did the French master realize all this? Or did he, a child of the Enlightenment, place at its limits his theory of shadow, distances, resistance, as just another way of comprehending nature which went back to paleontology, classification, and—may one say it?—mortification? By this last point I mean the demented search for the perfect specimen, as in museums of natural history which we passed through as children, but with what result, if not utter tedium? I have already spoken of the Deposition from the Cross as a pictorial convention, but is it not perhaps even more an extremely comprehensive study of those aspects which cannot be determined, which evade statics and gleam in the eye of a maid who wearily bends beneath the weight of the body?

Yet there is a path to salvation in such acts of classification; the catalogue rediscovers a secret and unexpected history of the image; its very artificiality becomes fantasy. Once everything has stopped forever, there is something to see: the little backgrounds of the yellowish photos, the unexpected appearance of an interior, the very dust on an image in which one recognizes the value of time.

Somehow I began to love this madness. It ordered the forms of existing energy; it kept them ready for who knows what upheavals.

For this reason, throughout my architectural development I have always been fascinated by museums. I clearly understood this fascination later—just when I plainly saw that museums bored me.

Many contemporary museums are cheats: often they try to distract the visitor, to render the whole thing charming, to create a spectacle. An analogous concept holds in the theater: a good drama does not necessarily need scenery or theatrical inventions; these belong to another type of spectacle which undoubtedly has its own seriousness, yet does not concern the theater any more than it does architecture. The theater is very similar to architecture because both involve an event—its beginning, development, and conclusion. Without an event there is no theater and no architecture. I refer, for example, to the procession in which Hamlet's body is carried away, or to Uncle Vanya's solitude, or to any two people who are talking in some house with hatred or with love, and of course to the grave. Are these events forms of functionalism, of necessity? I certainly do not think so; if the event is a good one, the scene will also be good, or it should be so.

And I believe that in this sense life is rather good; this is my realism, even if I do not know what type of realism it may be.

In fact, my relation to realism has always been quite singular. My project for the monument to the Resistance at Cuneo, done in 1962, has been considered a purist work, and in a way it is, yet this description seems strange to me. In any case, the project was rejected precisely because of its purism, which was judged impractical by a distinguished jury.

Notwithstanding this observation regarding a competition project, I do not want to go into my failures in this autobiography of my work; or rather I want only to mention and not discuss them. My most beautiful designs for competitions have always regularly been rejected. It would be easy but dishonest for me to blame inadequate support, factions, or friendships. My projects have been rejected not because of the political situation in Italy but because of their incomprehensibility or, more precisely, their impracticality. I am referring to projects like the monument for Cuneo, the Teatro Paganini at Parma, the residential complex in the San Rocco quarter of Monza, the town halls of Scandicci and Muggiò, the Palazzo della Ragione in Trieste, the student housing in Trieste, and finally the student housing at Chieti of 1976.

It is ironic to think that these very works later served as models for projects realized both in the schools and in practice; and perhaps it is doubly ironic, which is to say there is some justice, since a project like the one for the house at Borgo Ticino and others could only have appeared patently dishonest in the eyes of their owners, whether public or private.

When I was younger, around the time I was writing my first book, I used to apply a sentence from Nietzsche to human endeavor and also to architecture: "Where are those for whom they are working?" I am proud that I have not often built for people when I did not know where they were.

I believe it would be false to say that my disappointment was only with society. I am trying to avoid using too many literary quotations, but at times they are necessary. When I previously mentioned the comment made in the Osteria della Maddalena, I related it to a problem of engineering, of statics, to a midsummer afternoon, or to anything you wish, simply in order to express a certain condition; yet I also think it should be related to Lord Jim who, Conrad says, is one of us because "he had tumbled from a height he could

48

never scale again." I believe that for an engineer the meaning of such height cannot be better expressed: it is like that precipitous drop described in the conversation of the Osteria della Maddalena.

The Osteria della Maddalena no longer exists, nor does the Hotel Sirena, but does this not perhaps constitute part of our architectural education? Green stucco and the memory of the conversation just referred to offer us the only means possible—beyond the yardstick—to establish an architectural design.

But what was this yardstick? It may have been the acid green of the Hotel Sirena, perhaps incompatible with that rose rosanna—or Rossana, as the case may be—and with the harsh light of the lake, where the architecture, having abandoned form and function and the tastefulness so dear to bourgeois society, was merely a room in which the green was overwhelming, as in the altarpiece depicting the Deposition at Colmar, in which the rose was so delicate that it vanished in an anemic white.

Yet the architecture, having gone beyond function and history, dream and feeling, flesh and weariness, had approached a light that was rose-green, but filtered through so many things that it turned back into whiteness, or into the lake, or into the remoteness of the lake. This remoteness was almost like the forgetting of architecture, but it was also the place where the forgetting acquired an almost progressive meaning for me; it was like exploring one direction for so long that one forgot the premises; or like using some instrument which could reveal something more about the world, even if the meaning one wanted to know finally was not revealed, even if what remained was only the pleasure of the effort. We have tried to represent a precipitous place, a sheer drop in a legendary room, and even if we have not succeeded, the attempt is a great deal.

These unmeasurable heights and places do not belong merely to an oneiric world; the problem of measurement is one of the fundamental problems of architecture. I have always associated a rather complex meaning with the linear measure, particularly with an instrument like the yardstick, the folding wooden yardstick used by bricklayers. Without this yardstick there is no architecture; it is both an instrument and an apparatus, the most precise apparatus in architecture. This sense of measurement and distances made me especially fond of the investigation of topography made by Professor Golinelli at the Politecnico in Milan.

We used to spend entire mornings measuring the Piazza Leonardo da Vinci, perhaps the ugliest piazza in the world, but certainly the one most measured by generations of Milanese architects and engineers. Now it would happen that because the spring measurements were taking place with a certain laziness, and for a thousand other reasons which were not figured into the probabilities of inexactness, our triangulations often failed to close. The final form of the piazza became something absolutely original, and I found in this inability to close the triangulations not only our incompetency and indolence (of course), but also something mythical, like a further spatial dimension. Perhaps from these experiences my early projects for the bridge at the Triennale and the monument at Segrate were born. The unsuccessful attempt to close the triangle was an affirmation of a more complex geometry, which, however, proved

49

to be inexpressible and could demonstrate only the most elementary facts.

The union of different techniques resulting in a sort of realization-confusion has always impressed me. It has to do with the boundary between order and disorder; and the boundary, the wall, is a fact of mathematics and masonry. Thus the boundary or wall between city and non-city establishes two different orders. The wall can be a kind of graphic sign representing something like the difference between drawing and writing, or the meaning can emerge from the conjunction of the two. Perhaps the best example is Juan de la Cruz's drawing of Mount Carmel; I have drawn it myself over and over again in an attempt to understand it.

Reality and its description together form a complex binomial. Often an obsession exists which is superimposed on every other interest. Such obsessions are not always realized in the work, indeed they may never be realized, but they are among the most important intuitions, the secret code of other projects. During the last years of my stay in Zurich when I worked with Paul Hofer, I was completely preoccupied with the *castrum lunatum*, a crescent-shaped fort which Professor Hofer had discovered in the Roman cities in Switzerland, particularly Solothurn. The study of the *castrum lunatum* became the foundation for a project on the historic center of the city which, taking Roman typology as a point of departure, interpreted urban development in a new form.

It was an ambitious project, in which my passions for archaeology and the configuration of the city were united with a new attitude toward design. This union was never completely achieved, even though the efforts made by our group were in some way significant. I was enchanted by Solothurn, by its towers, river, bridges, the old buildings of gray stone. We pursued the crescent form in the foundations of houses, which were quite damp and chilly in cold Central Europe; I associated it with the shape of the moon that appeared over Solothurn during the cold nights, an association with Central Europe that also recurs in my memories of Colmar and Fribourg. Yet the *castrum lunatum* became increasingly inexpressible in architectural design or in any mode at all; perhaps it was the work of some Roman general who had envisaged this form because it provided a barrier which could not easily be traversed. Solothurn, like Nevers, Colmar, Trieste, was bound to a limit-point of architecture.

Years later, in the landscape of New England, I would discover a more remote yet likewise familiar difficulty, and some of my projects represent analogies with it.

I have always claimed that places are stronger than people, the fixed scene stronger than the transitory succession of events. This is the theoretical basis not of my architecture, but of architecture itself. In substance, it is one possibility of living. I liken this idea to the theater: people are like actors; when the footlights go up, they become involved in an event with which they are probably unfamiliar, and ultimately they will always be so. The lights, the music, are no different from a fleeting summer thunderstorm, a passing conversation, a face.

But at times the theater is closed; and cities, like vast theaters, sometimes are empty. While it may be touching that everyone acts out his little part, in the end, neither the mediocre actor nor the sublime actress is able to alter the course of events.

In my projects I have always thought about these things, and precisely in such a way as to attempt to structure the opposition between what is weak and what is strong. I mean this even in the sense of statics, of the strength of materials.

In describing architecture, I have always tried to refer the description back to the design. Actually, at this point it is easier for me to draw or, better, to employ that sort of graphic art which lies between drawing and writing, about which I spoke earlier. But in this book, when I have tried to describe a design, an urban house, a station, or whatever, I have always stopped myself at an uncertain dimension, by which I mean an unconstructible dimension.

I had thought of putting a description of several of my projects at the end of this scientific autobiography. (*A Few of My Projects* is in fact the title I prefer for my lectures, beginning with those I gave at the Federal Polytechnic Institute in Zurich. Heinrich Helfenstein translated this as *Einige meiner Entwuerfe*.) For the present book I thought of strictly limiting myself to "projects of affection." Thus I thought of beginning my catalogue with *Project for a Villa with Interior*. The nature of this project, which I already mentioned, is related, I believe, to its history and to a series of photographs of existing things, a range of reference of which the architect was conscious. The project was done in the autumn of 1978, and I consider it one of my best—as I usually consider my most recent projects.

The architectural drawings and the photographs are perhaps insignificant, yet the project itself represented the will no longer to draw architecture, but to recover it from things and from memory.

Actually, this project, like these notes, speaks of the dissolution of the discipline; it is not very different from the comments I made at the beginning of this text in reference to the day I observed the ancient bridge on the Mincio River. I am not sure how real this dissolution is. Perhaps it also is part of my awareness that great things are no longer possible and that the limitations of one's craft are a form of defense.

Otherwise we must transcend craft, which does not mean abandon it. In the modern period, however, this has rarely happened, although it can perhaps be seen in the architecture of men like Gaudì. The Güell Park in Barcelona always produces in me this sensation of disregarding the laws of statics and common sense, a creation of that forest of columns of which Hölderlin speaks. Boullée might also have had the idea of a forest full of columns, but perhaps not with the same obsessiveness.

In my recent writing, I have tried to explain all this by means of the idea of abandonment.

Actually, it was only a short time ago that I first visited the Abbey of San Galgano in Tuscany: this is perhaps the most convincing example of an architecture returned to nature, where abandonment is the beginning of design, where abandonment is identified with hope.

A scientific autobiography should talk more about my development as an architect, past as well as recent, yet I believe that these notes, extending from Santiago de Compostela to the bridge on the Mincio to San Galgano, effectively serve to express my active and theoretical participation in architecture. This participation is often identifiable in an object or in a piece of geography, in a domestic object or in a photo of the Parthenon or the Mosque of Bursa. These domestic and private journeys are public and scientific in the sense that today I find that all of my own past and present and every one of my drawings are worth even the most inattentive acknowledgement or observation.

It is difficult for me to compare myself with my contemporaries because I am increasingly aware of differences in place and time. This was my first intuition of the analogous city, and it was subsequently developed as a theory.

I believe that place and time are the first conditions of architecture and hence the most difficult. I have long had an interest in modern architecture, but I think that perhaps this style of architecture is linked in my mind with some buildings of my childhood—a villa or a residential block at Belo Horizonte in Brazil. This is a strange memory or experience of modern architecture, but it is also always accompanied by the awareness that aspects of reality can only be apprehended one at a time; I mean that rationality or the smallest degree of lucidity permits an analysis of what is certainly reality's most fascinating aspect: the inexpressible. Yet because of my health, education, or disposition, I have always mistrusted those who made of the irrational their own banner: they often seemed to me the most ill-equipped to do so, people who could not grasp the irrational at all. "Strolling one evening in a forest I happened to grasp the shadow of a plant": this passage from Boullée allowed me to understand the complexity of the irrational in architecture. On the other hand, it seemed to me that clothing designers, interior decorators, fashion photographers, were a many-colored fauna who had nothing at all to do with the irrational and the fantastic. Thus the housing and the district of Belo Horizonte, full of life, warmth—the warmth of life—repeated the rhythm of the Baroque cathedrals, that is, allowed things to happen; and this was an aspect of the architecture: not the beauty, not the Mosque of Bursa where I lost myself, but the continuation of the *insula*, the space of the people.

Perhaps this goal is really the preserve of the engineer; in reality, it is a very modest goal, but it is attained only with much difficulty.

So I drew the lighthouses of Massachusetts and Maine as objects of my own history, and it was my history, neither literary nor sentimental, which rose on this landscape with the tread of Ahab; and it was also the static quality of the place, its relation to the water, and the tower.

52

The more boundless an analogy, the more fixed it is, and in this duality lies a measured madness. I think I have listed a few built works which preoccupy me, like the Tempio Malatestiano in Rimini or Sant'Andrea in Mantua, because there is something in them which cannot be modified and which simultaneously re-engages time. The signs of people and objects that are without meaning, that supposedly are changeless—in fact they do change, but the change is always so terribly futile.

Change is within the very destiny of things, for there is a singular inevitability about evolution. Perhaps it has to do with the materials of objects and of human bodies, and hence of architecture. The singular authority of the built object and of the landscape is that of a permanence beyond people.

Although I have always desired to describe my projects, I do not know whether such description turns out better before or after the fact. It is like the testimony of a crime or a love affair. An architectural project is a vocation or a love affair; in either case, it is a construction. One can hold oneself back in the face of this vocation or affair, but it will always remain an unresolved thing. I have experienced this in the public gardens at Ferrara or Seville, where I have thought that any number of descriptions would have been valid; but in fact when I come to describe these gardens later, I have managed only to draw palms, especially with respect to Seville and the world of the Po, which is a mixture of real experience, image, and afternoons wasted in Ferrara or along the river itself.

This autobiography of my projects is the only means by which I can talk about them. I also know that one way or another it does not matter. Perhaps this again signifies forgetting architecture, and perhaps I have already forgotten it when I speak of the analogous city or when I repeat many times in this text that every experience seems definitive to me, that it is difficult for me to define a past and a future.

And if I have always claimed that everything is an unfolding or the opposite, whenever I actually see that theater on a raft rising from the water in the Venetian lagoon, I also see again the object at Modena or Cuneo. Yet is this stasis a condition of development? The compulsion to repeat also represents a lack of hope, but it now seems to me that to make the same thing again so that each time it turns out to be different is a difficult exercise, as difficult as looking at things and repeating them.

Of course, in an artist's or technician's development, things change as we ourselves change. But what does this change signify? I have always considered change a characteristic of cretins, a kind of stylishness—a stylishness characterized by inconsistency: as in the case of those who call themselves "modern" or "contemporary."

I have always loved the rigors of science, of repetition, and of the way in which all this ends up in isolation: just as conversely I have loved the ignorance and the intelligence of the tavern, the nonsense of a merry night.

It is certainly very difficult to establish or know the authentic boundaries of those things which I have called ignorant and intelligent: they too are like

53

geometric projections, like beauty and everything else. Once one departs from the norm or from the structure of things, it is certainly difficult to proceed; because of this, for many years I remained close to the discipline, to the classical treatises, to the rules, but not out of conformism or a need for order. In fact, if I were to paint a psychological portrait of myself, I would say that this tendency is stronger now, mainly because I have seen the often foolish limitations of whoever has departed from this order.

If one enters Sant'Andrea at Mantua on those days when the fog has penetrated the interior, one sees that no space so resembles the countryside, the Po lowland, as the measured and controlled space of this building. This is a theme which has always attracted me. This freedom compels me to maintain my love of order, or of a disorder that is always moderate and reasoned.

It is the freedom of the interrupted building, the abandoned palace, the village left in the mountains, the material which is deformed over time; the freedom of the original but also acquired nonsense of the Gonzaga palace outside of Mantua, together with the little artifices, restorations, systematizations of buildings: all this suggested a possible mode of being, like that of plastic flowers which preserve the rose by being different from it, by offering a different kind of beauty from that insisted upon by those who stupidly claim that beauty must always be newly born.

In the project for the municipal center at Florence, I imagined restored statues in the piazzas, like the alabaster Davids destined for tourists, thinking all the while that the copy is never entirely dissociated from the original, that in the plastic paintings of Venice with their ever-present lightbulb, hung in poor but decent kitchens among the family portraits, the mystery of the theater, whose performance is so important for us, is evoked again. We abhor directors who tamper with the text and ignore the period in which it was written; the ritual and hence the moment in which actions are performed constitute one of the fundamental rules of architecture and the theater.

This rule applies equally to the places of the city.

I thought about all these things during the Venetian autumn when I was observing the construction and birth of "the theater of the world." This unique building made me feel quite happy; in it I rediscovered the oldest threads of my experience and the more recent ones of my own history.

Perhaps I also saw rising from the water my projects for Modena and Cuneo which so resemble the cube-like theater, but as I have said, stasis had become a condition of my development. The compulsion to repeat may manifest a lack of hope, but it seems to me that to continue to make the same thing over and over in order to arrive at different results is more than an exercise; it is the unique freedom to discover.

In this light, ought I now to view my projects as a succession of unfinished and abandoned undertakings, or as a pursuit of the unexpected appearance of some new event? It seems to me that the event constitutes the novelty of a thing, and it is in this context that I have spoken of a competition, a particular place, a moment.

Regarding the project for the villa in the Ticino, I spoke of a condition of
54

happiness: is happiness perhaps a technique? Certainly the feeling of happiness cannot be transmitted except by way of some personal experience or some event; the event, on the other hand, is transmitted through a work. Perhaps only the most academic minds are indifferent to the role of events in life, yet very few people know how to express them.

What surprises me most in architecture, as in other techniques, is that a project has one life in its built state but another in its written or drawn state.

At this point I should speak of my built works, which up to now have not been many. Still, they constitute perhaps the central point of this biography or autobiography, for I identify them with a part of myself.

There is no photograph of Fagnano Olona that I love so much as the one of the children standing on the stair under the huge clock which is indicating both a particular time and also the time of childhood, the time of group photos, with all the joking that such photos usually entail. The building has become pure theater, but it is the theater of life, even if every event is already anticipated.

Because every aspect of the building is anticipated, and because it is precisely this anticipation that allows for freedom, the architecture is like a date, a honeymoon, a vacation—like everything that is anticipated so that it can occur. Although I also love what is uncertain, I have always thought that only small-minded people with little imagination are opposed to discreet acts of organization; for it is only such efforts of organization that in the end permit contretemps, variations, joys, disappointments. Nonetheless, it remains true that I envisaged this theater-school in terms of everyday realities, and the children who were playing there comprised the house of life, as opposed to that other project of mine, the house of death, the cemetery at Modena. Yet even the latter has its own life and is affected by the passage of time: still far from being completed, it emerges unexpectedly in yellowed photographs, in wax flowers, in the devotions of the living, in the unexpected play of light during the cold and heat of the seasons.

Between the houses of childhood and death, between those of play and work, stands the house of everyday life, which architects have called many things—residence, habitation, dwelling, etc.—as if life could develop in one place only. Through my own life or craft I have partly lost this concept of the fixed place, and at times I superimpose different situations and different times, as my reader has already seen. Precisely this tendency has led me to reconsider "my country," that is, the concept of my country. This seems to me very important for the understanding of architecture.

Of course, "my country" may be nothing more than a street or a window; and while it may be difficult to recover one's "homeland" once it has been lost, the concept need not contradict the notion of the citizen of the world, the *Welt-bürger* proclaimed by Goethe. But it is difficult to express this concept, which in fact led me to the idea of the *Project for a Villa with Interior*.

I must say that better than all else I love the little modifications of a certain house on a certain lake, where the architecture or the totality of things that makes up the house is necessarily based on life: because of functional considerations, because of an imponderable element which overlays the people sitting around the table, making it seem as if they existed in a continuous present.

There the great granite table, my most recent construction, is still the beautiful piece of stone that my friend removed from the quarry. The very house itself, with all its objects and instruments and furnishings, is also an apparatus by definition and necessity—if only because of its existence in time. And it is as much an apparatus of death as one of life.

I seem to understand my completed projects better, or I am able to complete them better the farther their original intentions recede into the past.

In my attachment to the image, it often seems to me that to express the life of this image or thing or situation or person requires a kind of condition of interference. That is, everything becomes representable once desire is dead— to use a phrase that can lend itself to many interpretations. Almost paradoxically, whenever there is a loss of desire, the form, the project, the relation, love itself, are cut off from us and so can be represented. I do not know how much of this is cause for joy or for melancholy, but I am certain that desire is something that exists beforehand or that lives in a general sense; it cannot coexist with any design process or ritual. At times I think that the best situation is always that of experiencing something after desire is dead; for this reason I have always loved unbuilt projects, like the one for the theater in Parma, where I settled in advance on an exercise which would be perfect in itself, where every discovery would be pure technical refinement, where the causes of the action would be, so to speak, unveiled. Here I am reminded of the construction of the Sacri Monti and also of the repetition of scenes which portray an emotion, but where it is always one that is anticipated. In *Don Giovanni*, Mozart's reference to another of his works does not so much represent the sign of his own imprisonment in the compulsion to repeat as a degree of freedom. Thus I like to quote from objects or even events in my own life, as well as describe or study or illuminate something whose direct bearing on my work is not obvious.

At times I have applied this method to various works of architecture, and besides my theory of architecture and the city, this principle of description has been for me a formative fact of the first order. I still try to follow it, even if things tend to change slightly and my previous descriptions may have been expressed in the architecture of others.

Below I quote a brief description of the Duomo in Milan taken from my blue notebooks. The description is from 1971, and it often seems to me to resemble one of my projects. In effect, it shows how every work we experience becomes our own:
"Noteworthy experience of the architecture of the Duomo in Milan; I have not climbed to the top for some time now. It relates to the problem of the alignment of elements and, naturally, to verticality. Having gone up the stair, one walks down a long open-air passageway. The passageway cuts through the flying buttresses by means of narrow rectangular doorways which follow

one another with the rhythm of the buttresses. These flying structures help drain the water from the nearly flat roof by conducting it to the gargoyles at the perimeter. The roof plane is like a little stone piazza. Study the dimensions of the stone. On the sides of the building the scale of the architecture is given by the flying buttresses and by the base. The base is a notable example of *contaminatio* in architecture, and its like is not found in any other Gothic work. (In fact, this work demonstrates the utter inadequacy of that stylistic label.) In substance, it is not very different from the stylobates which surround the Temple of Fortuna Virilis or the temples of Augustus at Nîmes and at Pola in Yugoslavia, as well as many others (Rocco, notes on the sources of the Duomo). The buttresses at ground level are in regular succession and can be seen as rectangular volumes which divide the sides into equal sections. They weigh heavily on the base, which is continuous. The entry of worshippers through the facade is incredible: the solution is in the scale of the doors and in the agitated quality of the enclosed elements. Only such agitation could somehow relate to the multitude of elements in the cathedral. Red and blue paintings and hangings are put up on the facade during religious holidays."

These stylistic elements do not detract from the character of the great building; in fact, they augment it: the Duomo is the *fabrica del dôm*, and hence the architecture, like the *cà grande*, is above all the house which is constructed for everyone. Therefore it cannot be finished.

This structure, which is at its base almost elementary, affords the possibility of moving inside and over the city; the walk on the roof of the Duomo in fact constitutes an important experience of urban architecture. For my own part, I have long been impressed with those equal volumes on the side of the building; they reappear in the central street of my projects for Modena and for Fagnano Olona. Those volumes create a typical street condition, which is in turn disrupted by a multitude of things, for example the statues and spires which culminate at street level in a Roman base that is continuous, high, and distinct like a tiny autonomous structure. Often while looking at it I have asked myself, what other temple could such a base support? Perhaps, I think, the one envisaged by pilgrims with the agitation of its great enclosed elements. This agitation, which is very evident on the brick facade—a sort of vertical section that seems unfinished—was the only solution possible in a building which really could not be finished.

This idea of the unfinished or abandoned followed me everywhere, but it is a totally different notion from that which prevails in modern art. For me, the abandoned object contains an element of destiny, more or less historical, as well as a kind of equilibrium. I recognized it in the very definition of the duomo as the *fabrica del dôm*, and here *fabrica*, in my opinion, is meant not so much in the classical, Albertian sense as in the sense of a thing which is in the process of being made or which is made without any specific end. These unfinished architectural sections reappear in the *fabrica* of the student housing at Chieti; here too I realized that the building, in order to correspond to the changes of life, had to fabricate life and be fabricated out of it.

But there is also a singular beauty in those brick walls which mark the limits of a house. The most impressive examples of this are certainly the Brantmauer in Berlin, often black and furrowed by pipes like wounds, and similarly the buildings on Broadway in New York, where the cornices are broken, clearly revealing their sections, their design. In New York it is precisely the appli-

19 "La Favorita," near Mantua.

cation of Beaux-Arts architecture on a giant scale that produces these abnormal effects of solid and ruined architecture, unexpected types, a beauty which we already look at with an archaeological eye, a beauty made of ruins, collapses, superimpositions.

I tried to express this concept of emotion in several of my New York drawings, for example in "Collapses of the Earth" in 1977. I do not want to interpret these drawings here because I wish to avoid becoming facile and mechanical, but there is no doubt that in them the personal, almost private element is accompanied by an inquiry into an architecture which is not necessarily in ruins, but in which, as I have written at the bottom of one drawing, the images follow different directions, or are superimposed, because of the ways the land settles. The images are those of repetition, of empty or abandoned houses, of tangles of iron which no longer support anything. However, in "Other Conversations" from 1978, the architectural order is sustained as if by pillars, streets, bridges. Naturally, the significance of the "Other Conversations" escapes the general public; yet it seems to be carved upon the stones of a hypothetical dam.

Recalling the city still suggests to me a reading not only of my own architecture but indeed of architecture in general. I believe that I have access to a privileged way of looking, of observing. It is a position that is closer to the engineer's than to that of the psychologist or geographer: I like to apprehend a structure in its broad outlines and then think how these lines intersect. This is no different from the experience of life and relationships: the nucleus of a fact is always rather simple, and indeed, the more simple a fact is, the more it is destined to clash with the events which it itself produces. I am reminded of a sentence from Hemingway which I found frightening yet fascinating: "All truly wicked things are born from an innocent moment." I am not interested in commenting on this sentence, which has the glibness of most beautiful statements. Still, it is important to me to recognize this nucleus in order to know to what extent its developments are, so to speak, internal and to what extent they are induced externally. And by developments I mean deformations, collapses, changes.

Ever since I was a boy I have been interested in these important ideas, which seemed to me to explain even the peripheral characters in a play; I have been interested, that is, in how bodies and materials react to their own development. There is something analogous in architecture, for example, in colonial architectures: one of the facts which profoundly impressed me in Brazil was the visible transformation of men and things from their original nucleus. I was impressed by a church in Ouro Prieto where the *retablo* appeared to be a foreground more than a background. It was in fact a facade that one entered from behind, like a stage; in other words, the *retablo* was formed by actual stages at different heights, a fact which also presupposed different entrances into the church.

I can imagine the historical and sociological observations that might be made with regard to this, but what I found important, apart from the typological invention itself, was the deformation of the central nucleus, which was, in this case, the plan of the church.

61

In my early youth this same interest compelled me to try to understand questions of biology and chemistry, because I had always thought that the human mind and body were closely linked to the imagination. Today I am still much more interested in any kind of medical book than in psychological texts, especially the literary psychology which has been fashionable in recent years. In addition, the idea of explaining illnesses according to psychological factors has always seemed to me a dubious approach; illness is due to a series of defenses and resistances in a material, and depends on both the original nature of that material and its history, or the mechanism of its history.

Thus in the past few years I have been particularly interested in books about immunology. Ivan Roitt's definition in *Essential Immunology* deeply impressed me: "Memory, specificity, and the recognition of 'non-self'—these lie at the heart of immunology." Memory and specificity as characteristics enabling the recognition of the self and of what is foreign to it seem to me the clearest conditions and explanations of reality. Specificity can not exist without memory, nor can memory that does not emanate from a specific moment: only the union of the two permits the awareness of one's own individuality and its opposite (of *self* and *non-self*).

For several years these ideas have seemed to answer my questions, seemed to correspond to my interest in things and, let us also say, my interest in architecture. Memory is constructed out of its own specificity, and whether this construction is defensible or not, it can recognize alien structures. This is also man's relation with the city, with the construction of his microclimate, with his own specificity.

Even though I have always been quite involved with things, I have for some time abandoned those which were alien to me: my search is perhaps only what Stendhal has called the search for happiness, and it leads me to a place which is not the place of the possible but the place of the actual event.

I continue to look at things in this way, yet this very fixation enables me to develop my individual abilities and permits me to arrive at new solutions.

What solutions? For example, in the competitions for the Palazzo della Ragione and for the student housing at Trieste in 1974, many themes alien to the city were accumulated, so to speak, within the body of the buildings. I could speak of my relationships with cities just as I do my relationships with people, but in a certain sense the former are richer because they also include people. This is particularly true when a certain event has occurred in a city. These relationships become fixed in a memory, and memory soon becomes symbol: for example, before the present tourist boom, there used to be yellowed photographs of honeymoons, generally spent in Venice, which could be seen decorating the sideboards of kitchens or living rooms. These points of connection between personal and public history have always appeared to me laden with significance. Today I love to collect albums of these photographs, which, however, have become devalued as a result of those glossy manufactured photographs of commercial publishers which we find so distasteful.

The project for the student housing followed by at least ten years a rather intense period during which I often stayed in Trieste. This earlier period was

20 *Palm tree by the lake.*

precisely like the old photographs, except that it continued to grow in me like a sentiment which over time accumulated many things. Between the student housing at Trieste and that at Chieti, furthermore, two years passed; and despite the different results obtained in the two projects, there are in both analogies associated with my experience.

To study the Trieste student housing, we went back to the old psychiatric hospital which bordered the site for the competition and which was still open at the time. I recall that my encounter with this quite freely organized community was truly unique—much more interesting than what is usually called the "site analysis." Among my passions for public things I have a great respect for, and perhaps I can even say I have participated in, the authentic liberation of some ancient places of the abuse of power. The abuse of the mind has always seemed to me worse than that of the body, even if the two, as we know, are often joined. Well, in my encounter with the people at this place, I remember very well that from the beginning there was a mutual uneasiness: it was an uncomfortable situation, even frightening, to be honest. But at once we realized, much more vividly than can be argued in books, that this fear was simply the result of the correspondence which was rapidly emerging between two different forms of behavior. I do not believe I am digressing too far from my architecture and from the work I am discussing; for to understand architecture we must also go beyond it to questions of behavior, of education, to a whole set of questions that I would like to call stylistic. By this term I do not mean architectural style in the purely technical sense (e.g., Doric or Corinthian), but the impact which great buildings have on us and on history. Thus many people who fail to perceive this distinction are amazed that I admire certain of Gaudi's works like the Güell Park, while other works, much more like my own, do not interest me. This perhaps became clearer in the project for Chieti.

Now, while we talked with the patients of the mental hospital, the project for the student housing became bound up with Trieste, and the young students and the ex-patients who had to be reestablished in a new house in turn became merged with the city architecture. The project formed a bridge between the city of Trieste and the strong, rugged terrain which allowed the sea to penetrate as far as the karst formation. Few cities can be comprehended from above as Trieste can, just as in few other cities can one walk along the harbor and go out on the piers with such a sense of festivity. Perhaps one can in New York near the West Side Highway, where I have recently completed an analogous project with my students. Certainly it is analogous in terms of its differences: in New York the old wood and iron piers enter the Hudson and are separated from the city by the old and often collapsed highways. This is what I have called a zone of industrial archaeology, once again using the term in a sense that is different from general usage. In a project designed with students in New York, houses are built on the piers, and at times the old buildings are left standing, long warehouses of iron and brick with incredible Palladian heads. This is similar to the project in Trieste which is concentrated in the higher part of the city. The line of the karst plateau corresponds to the skyline of New York, a city which is something like a mountain with stratifications where the built structures represent, more than anywhere else, the social, ethnic, and economic tangle of the city.

The comparison of these cities is not so unusual, not only because in both there is the presence of the sea, but also because both are related to that primordial city built on the sea, Venice.

I try never to speak of Venice, even though it is one of the places where I have taught and hence lived for nearly twelve years. It is also strange that even though many events have been resolved for me in Venice, I still feel a relative stranger to the city—more so certainly than I do to Trieste or New York or many other cities.

Yet now I speak of Venice because it is the setting of my latest project: the floating theater designed for the 1979–80 Biennale. I love this work very much, and I might also say that it expresses a moment of happiness; perhaps it happens that all works, insofar as they express a moment of creation, belong to that strange sphere which we call happiness. I shall speak of this work here, but I shall also want to return to it later in describing several other projects. I should like to say immediately that in this case the work has made a great impression on me through its life, that is, through its evolution, its construction, and its position in the city, and also through the spectacles performed in it. While I was listening to some music by Benedetto Marcello on opening night and watching people flowing up the stairs and crowding onto the balconies, I perceived an effect which I had only vaguely anticipated. Since the theater stood on the water, one could see from its window the *vaporetti* and boats passing by just as if one were standing on another boat; and these other boats entered into the image of the theater, constituting a scene that truly was both fixed and mobile. In an essay on this building where he took up my comment about the influence of the architecture of the light-house along the Maine coast, Manfredo Tafuri said that the lighthouse or beacon, here seen more properly as a house of light, is made for observing but also for being observed. And this observation has suggested to me an interpretation for many works of architecture: every tower is made for observing, but even more for being observed. My drawings entitled "The Window of the Poet," in which the idea of the library in the school at Fagnano Olona was further extended, involved this sort of observation from the interior out to a landscape where one could also, but not necessarily, be observed. And what better place for a beacon, a house of light, literally a lighthouse, than by the sea, in a border zone between sea and land, amid beach, rock, sky, and clouds? Perhaps this was and is my America—the white houses of New England, the boats, the Maine that I had already envisaged in my adolescent reading, where the house was the Pequod and the meaning of the search could only be a white object, which is also laden with the past but perhaps already and forever devoid of desire. From boyhood I have believed that Ahab too worked at his trade without desire, for lack of desire was a necessity.

And all this was conveyed in nothing but the white of the house, the sea, the village, the monster.

The widows' walks on the houses in New England recall the Greek ritual of scanning the sea for what does not return—a substitution of ritual for pain, just as obsession is a substitution for desire. Similarly the repetition of the form of the tympanum on a building does not cause the event itself to recur. The event might not ever happen anyway. I am more interested in the preparations, in what *might* happen on a midsummer night. In this way,

65

architecture can be beautiful before it is used; there is beauty in the wait, in the room prepared for the wedding, in the flowers and the silver before High Mass.

This was the way I first thought of the Little Scientific Theater, and my idea was bound up with the drama *Die nicht Versöhnt* [*The Unreconciled*], so-called because it was intended for those who could not be reconciled after some event, and perhaps above all for those who could not be reconciled to the fact that there had been no event at all. *The Unreconciled* is not necessarily the other side of *The Reunited*, although I loved to see these two dramas performed together.

"Non-reconciliation" can suggest a mode of being. And here my architecture rose and fell: I no longer pursued analogies like the images on cards—King, Knave, Fool, Knight—but instead recomposed a world where things contrasted with each other.

Yet *inside* and *outside* are also part of the meaning of the theater, and I rediscovered the other meaning of the seashell, "daughter of stone and the whitening sea," which Alcaeus had written about and which perhaps drew me to architecture just as it "astonishes the minds of children."

Astonishment has a hard crust made of stone and shaped by the sea, like the crust of the great constructions of steel, stone, and cement which form the city.

From these things I learned about architecture, and I made the same drawings over and over, searching for the web of connections in the life of man.

Transcending specific analogies, I saw more and more clearly how much beauty lies in the place where matter encounters different meanings. Nothing can be beautiful, not a person, a thing, or a city, if it signifies only itself, indeed, if it signifies nothing but its own use. With this recognition I went beyond the most banal and commonplace aspects of architecture: the old truths of the classical treatise-writers filtered through nineteenth-century positivism, the over-refined beauty of functions divested of referential images, signifiying only themselves.

Perhaps I considered all this while I gazed from the balcony of the Venetian theater, overlooking the Doges' Palace. Venice was receding into a quite mysterious sea, and the gold sphere of the Dogana could be only the beginning and end of every voyage. Like the ships in the harbor, the theater also arrived from the sea and stood in the lagoon: José Charters wrote to me that the thing which most struck him was precisely this impression, that the theater had come from the sea, and that it constituted a boundary between sea and land. It reminded him that every good thing comes from the sea, and he also recalled his own country and how the Portuguese national poet had often said: "Portugal is that country which is found where the land ends and the sea begins."

It also seemed to me that the theater was in a place where architecture ended and the world of the imagination or even the irrational began. This is how I looked at the mysterious verdigris figures who bear and play with the golden sphere, while I focused on the articulation of their joints and the slow movements of the figure of Fortuna. The joints seemed like bizarre wounds worked into the metal, the mended parts of a unique body which was the result of sinister surgical experiments, even more sinister than that always sinister process of turning the human body into a statue. They arose from a garden, green figures of verdigris and green vegetation, and were strange as green figures always are, and they also brought to mind the yellowish-green grass that grows between the gray stones of the cathedrals near the sea or the ocean in Galicia, Portugal, Brittany. These figures also reminded me of one of my favorite facades, that of Santa Clara at Santiago de Compostela, which contains a little statue of the saint in a dark stone wall furrowed with green, a green tint the color of verdigris, which seems to trickle from an internal crack, curiously cleansing. And at the center stands the little saint, completely painted like a precious doll abandoned in an inaccessible place—just as the Venetian Fortuna is inaccessible and perhaps not much noticed as it slowly moves: for it is essential that no one detect the movements of fortune.

The Venetian green contrasts with the cold color of the iron on the roof of my theater. This metal is reflected in the gray of the lagoon, while above it stands the ball and the slowly creaking metal banner. Here again is Hölderlin's "*im Winde / Klirren die Fahnen,*" yet this time an almost abstract creaking, precisely like that of the ships docked in the harbor.

What pleases me above all is that the theater is a veritable ship, and like a ship, it is subject to the movements of the lagoon, the gentle oscillations, the rising and sinking; so that in the uppermost galleries a few people might experience a slight sea-sickness that proves distracting and is increased by the sight of the water line, which is visible beyond the windows. I cut these windows according to the level of the lagoon, the Giudecca, and the sky. The shadows from the little crosses of the window mullions stand out against the wood, and these windows make the theater resemble a house. Moreover, like a lighthouse, the theater is a place where one can be observed as well as observe. The beacon, the lighthouse, the house of light, are structures for the sea and of the sea, and I have seen ancient ones made of wood, often of whitened wood, which merge with the white ocean off the coast of Maine. I always go to visit lighthouses: once at Cabe Espichel in Portugal we stood near the huge light until it was turned on at dusk. The horizontal rotary movement made by the light is very impressive and is seen best by standing next to it, where one can grasp the sense of the machine: this effect is lost at great distances. These observations are important for architecture, just as the ancients observed the course of the stars and Giuseppe Piermarini studied clocks.

The tower of my Venetian theater might be a lighthouse or a clock; the campanile might be a minaret or one of the towers of the Kremlin: the analogies are limitless, seen, as they are, against the background of this preeminently analogous city. I think it was at Izmir that I watched and heard the awakening minarets in insomniac dawns; in Moscow, I experienced the *frisson* of the Kremlin's towers and sensed the world of the Mongols and of wooden watchtowers set on some boundless plain—I sensed things in this way far more than as elements reducible to those we call architecture.

Indeed there are a great many things that it is useless to probe further, like the writing in drawings, the light in a portrait, the forgetting of a photograph which dates back to a memory; and certainly we are only able to evaluate those operations which have reached their completion.

Several people have spoken of the light of Carpaccio in connection with the interior of my theater. I do not wish to take up the often very beautiful comments of the critics and of all those who have taken an interest in this building, but I would like to recall one of Mazzariol's, in which he speaks of a pre-monumental Venice, a Venice not yet white with the stone of Sansovino and Palladio. It is the Venice of Carpaccio, and I see it in the interior light, in the wood, and I am reminded of certain Dutch interiors which evoke ships and are near the sea.

This Venice of wood is also closely related to the Po delta as well as to the bridges which cross the Venetian canals, of which the Accademia bridge, although of course a nineteenth-century construction, offers a better idea than the Rialto. But the rediscovery of this Venice was possible only through the intervention of some precise, discreetly colored object, representing an elementary but sure technology—for example, a barge or, indeed, a theatrical machine.

As for my other *teatrino*, Rafael Moneo has called this Little Scientific Theater "the Milanese machine," and strangely enough, it preceded the Venetian theater almost by chance. It was especially concerned with those mechanisms which are most properly theatrical—the stage, curtain, lights, scenery. In itself it was a box with a tympanum which recalled, as I have said, the theater of Roussel, the Po theaters, the white theater of my childhood. The beauty of this little theater resides in its atmosphere, what I have called the magic of the theater. In the Venetian theater, on the other hand, the magic is created by an unusual mixture of typologies: the amphitheater and the galleries, the visible staircases, a stage where the central stage-set is a little window from which one can see the Giudecca canal. Thus the actor is also part of the audience.

Anthony Vidler has given me a copy of Frances Yates's *Theatre of the World* with a beautiful dedication: "For A., from the theater of memory to the theater of science." Certainly the Little Scientific Theater was the theater of memory, but memory in the sense of repetition: this was its magic. The Venetian theater is of course closer to the anatomical theater at Padua and to Shakespeare's Globe Theatre (and the "Globe" was in fact literally the "Theater of the World" as, going back to the Venetian tradition, this project of mine has been called the *teatro del mondo*).

I was interested in how the anatomical theaters and the Globe Theatre made the human figure central as in fact all small amphitheaters do. The Roman theater, on the other hand, had a fixed back wall, and this wall was comparable to the *retablo* in the Spanish churches, which serves as both the altar and the backdrop for liturgical action. Yet in the amphitheater a back wall was not necessary because all the interest was focused on the play and principally on the animal, man or beast. The same thing was true of the anatomical theater, where the boards of the stage, because of the focus of the action, rose mechanically from below with the cadaver. Here too was the body of a man, a

68

man already deposed, painstakingly studied by a still humanistic science. Actually, the actors were not viewed differently in the Globe Theatre.

But my Venetian theater is distinguished from these others by the fact that the stage is a corridor which joins a door and a window. It has no centrality on the ground level; the centrality exists in the circulation of the balconies and in the incline of the pointed roof. I liked the idea of this interior incline so much that I built a structure in which common elements and joints were disengaged as in a temporary construction, and this in fact is what gives the theater its temporary appearance. Thus, in the structure the rods and brass joints, which look almost gilded, move closer together and become superimposed, creating a skeleton, a machine, a living device that no longer has its original shape and cannot be compared to a scaffold. Iron and wood become two parallel structures, recalling for me the onion-shaped sections of Byzantine domes and the narrow towers or minarets where the interior and exterior are two complementary but not necessarily distinct architectures.

The metal plating of these towers and domes; the iron, copper, lead, the stone itself; the stone pinnacles of the Duomo at Modena which bear on an irregular structure; the verdigris which trickles down the white stone from the immense domes; and, above all, those steeples on the Gothic campaniles sharpened to absurd extremes, green against the white of the sky: I studied all these from the window of my office at the Federal Polytechnic Institute in Zurich, especially the steeple of the Frauenkirche.

In old engravings one can see the Limmat which flows through Zurich. The surrounding countryside is dotted with wooden mills that are topped with pointed roofs, green as verdigris or leaden-colored, covered with black steel or iron. The interiors and exteriors of this Gothic city must not have been different from the Venice of Carpaccio. Nor from Dutch, Norman, or Oriental cities: they must have resembled those Persian carpets in the canvases of Dutch painters which cover tables and display their Oriental colors in the Nordic light of a low window. One has the sense of the interior of a city which escapes every simplification.

In *The Architecture of the City*, I spoke apprehensively, almost fearfully, of the remains of houses destroyed by the war. I saw pink walls, hanging sinks, tangles of pipes, destroyed intimacies; I so vividly imagined the feeling and the vague malaise of these destroyed apartments that a certain idea for a "project with interior" has followed me ever since. In designing the Venetian theater I knew from the start that this idea was the life or silence of the theater: the silence of the theater is like the silence of empty churches.

The houses of the dead and those of childhood, the theater or the house of representation—all these projects and buildings seem to me to embrace the seasons and ages of life. Yet they no more represent themes than functions; rather they are the forms in which life, and therefore death, are manifested.

I could speak in this sense of still other projects which I have so far barely touched upon, projects like the housing block at San Rocco and that for the

*21 Brant Point lighthouse,
Nantucket.*

Gallaratese quarter in Milan. The first dates back to 1966; the second to 1969–1970. Concerning the former I have mentioned only the superimposition of the Roman grid and the subsequent shifting of this grid, creating an effect like the accidental crack in a mirror. Concerning the latter, I have mentioned its size and simplicity, in the sense of a rigorous technology.

Yet in speaking of the forms in which human life is manifested, I ought to elaborate further on some of those structures with which this sense of life has been associated for me and which have impressed me from an archaeological and anthropological point of view ever since my early youth. I have mentioned the *corrales* of Seville, the courtyards of Milan, in particular the courtyard of the Hotel Sirena; and the balconies, arcades, corridors, as well as the literary and actual impressions made on me by convents, schools, barracks. In a word, those forms of dwelling—together with that of the villa—are stored in the history of man to such a degree that they belong as much to anthropology as to architecture. It is difficult to imagine other forms, other geometric representations, precisely because we do not already have examples of them.

In *The Concept of Mind*, Gilbert Ryle asserts that "analogy is constituted by things that have already been apprehended by means of a process of which only the result is reported. . . . Multiplications have to be done before they can be marked 'correct'. . . . 'Contours are abstractions' or 'Contour lines are abstract map-symbols' is a proper and useful instruction for a map-referee to give to would-be readers and makers of maps. 'Contour lines are the outward expressions of the mapmakers' mental acts of conceiving heights (in feet) above sea-level' suggests that reading a map entails penetrating the impenetrable shadow-life of some anonymous surveyor." This passage has always seemed quite important to me, not only for architecture, but for the sciences, arts, and technologies as well. Here the idea of analogy is represented in a way that is very different from Jung's definition, which I have written about elsewhere: it refers to things we know nothing more of than the result, just as the contour lines refer only to the actual, if impenetrable, life of an anonymous surveyor.

This is one meaning of the project which has always interested me particularly, and which perhaps gives a meaning to these notes of mine. Like an error in measurement, which I spoke of earlier, the analogy is an acquisition of something about which only the result is known. In other words, it seems to me that with every process only the end result may really be known, and by process I also mean every project. Thus describing a project before it is completed is like providing the thread of a process which has no conclusion.

I believe that for certain kinds of artists, the origins of things are corroded and destroyed by the actuality of places. I often forget voices and superimpose different people on the same backgrounds, the same places—not entirely unconsciously, because I think that it is probably necessary to ignore many things.

The autobiography of a project is certainly only in the project itself, and describing it is a form of communicating that is not different from designing or building. In recent years, I have read many things about my work—often the most strange and disparate things—and I cannot say, as one often does in such cases, that I have learned anything. I have learned only that many opinions are valid, even when they do not coincide with what the artist had in mind.

I always think of a place in a particular way. Certainly in any given place many things come together; a place presents itself as a result of many observations: the panorama from the balcony, the flowing water, the drift of the conversation, the gestures, and all those things that we call "love." Perhaps only through a kind of inattention, the most benevolent form of betrayal, is one faithful to a place, to what ultimately changes very slowly.

Every midsummer evening has its companionship and its solitude, and the architect or the playwright must grasp the broad outlines of a scene quickly, because he knows that the characters and even their feelings may change, or that in any case the representation will be different in time.

All this allows for the representation of the past with the desire of the present. What frightens me most is the past of a man in whom desire is dead: for someone in this state, the past paradoxically glows with the colors of the future, with those of hope. None of my projects turns away from the past, perhaps because I have never been able to express all the joy for the future which a project, an object, a journey, a person could possess for me. I do not know how much of this is joy or is in fact melancholy, but it seems to me a condition for living and working at one's craft.

Without desire no certainty remains, and the imagination itself is reduced to a commodity. Yet that familiar little scene, with its discreet lights and shadows, its increasingly decayed and corroded monuments, the very bones of the grave, and every apparent novelty which in the end is always old, is still something which we can recount, even repetitively. For we know how much the unforeseeable is foreseen; yet we also know how unforeseen are the effects of that potential energy which lies latent, determining the contours of human life, the light and shadow, and the certain consummation or consumption of human bodies.

Because of this, the building of a place that is relatively permanent yet receptive to personal modifications is still something that I can accept within a limited disorder of things; for it is somehow honest, and it responds to our aspirations.

In this way it seems to me possible to go beyond every superficial avant-garde. This may also be the significance of several of my drawings made between 1974 and 1980. I am fond of titles like "Other Conversations" and "The Time of an Event." These drawings were like a concentrated and synoptic screenplay of a film: I saw the images of "The Time of an Event" as the frames of a possible film which I have had in mind for some time now.

My only experience with film occurred at the 1973 Triennale in Milan. The film had the title of Loos's beautiful essay on architecture, "Ornament and Crime," and it was a collage of architectural works and pieces of different films which tried to introduce the discourse of architecture into life and at the same time view it as a background for human events. From cities and palaces we passed to excerpts from Visconti, Fellini, and other directors. Venice, and the problem of the historical urban center, acquired further significance as a background to the impossible love described by Visconti in *Il Senso*. I recall a white, desperate Trieste which only the story of Italo Svevo's *Senility* made

72

*22 Venetian skyline. Photograph by
Antonio Martinelli.*

clear, especially its architectural context. We later shot the final part of the film on the outskirts of Milan at dawn. I truly believe that I had gone beyond architecture, or at least explained it better. The problem of technique also vanished, and now I think that the realization of this film may be the continuation of so many things I am seeking in architecture.

This film also contained some of my love for my theater in Venice, for it was an anomalous work, presenting itself with the same imposing quality and fragility that a machine possesses. A number of critics have stated that my works resemble stage designs, and I have responded that they do have this resemblance just like the architecture of Palladio, Schinkel, Borromini—just like all architecture. I do not intend to defend myself here from any charges, but it occurs to me now that I have never understood how I can be accused of such different things as producing works which are scenographic and which at the same time display a kind of poverty of expressive means.

But this has little importance for me now. I believe I have made it clear that I consider any technique possible; I would go so far as to claim that a method or technique can be a style. To consider one technique superior to, or more appropriate than, another is a sign of the madness of contemporary architecture and of the Enlightenment mentality which the architectural schools have transmitted wholesale to the Modern Movement in architecture.

I must say that I have always had an ambivalent attitude toward modern architecture—and quite unwillingly. I made a thorough study of it at the start of my career, especially in relation to the city, and so when I recently saw the vast working-class neighborhoods in Berlin, particularly Berlin-Britz, and in Frankfurt, I felt a great admiration for the building of these new cities. But as I have already said, I have always completely rejected the whole moralistic and petit-bourgeois aspect of modern architecture. This has been clear to me since the beginning of my studies, especially because of my admiration for Soviet architecture: I think that so-called Stalinist architecture—a term which I use in a purely chronological sense—was abandoned for no reason. This abandonment was a capitulation to the culture of modern architecture, whose utter failure we see today not only in Europe but in every country throughout the world.

I should say, though, that I have always loved a few modern architects, principally Adolf Loos and Mies van der Rohe, and I still consider myself their student. They are the architects who have done most to establish a thread of continuity with their history and hence with human history. In *The Architecture of the City*, they served to help me demolish functionalist culture in a meaningful way, and I quoted what they said to this purpose. Here the question of "personality" also counts for something, and it is certainly very important that Loos is not represented merely by his architecture, and that "Ornament and Crime" remains an extremely beautiful title for an architectural essay because it alludes only indirectly to architecture. Mies, on the other hand, is the only one who knew how to make architecture and furniture which transcend time and function.

I do not wish to treat here other questions related to function: it is evident that every object has a function to which it must respond, but the object does not end at that point because functions vary over time. This has always been a rather scientific assertion of mine, and I have extracted it from the history

74

of the city and of human life: from the transformations of a palace, an amphi-theater, a convent, a house, or of their various contexts. I have dealt with this subject in relation to monuments in *The Architecture of the City*. I have seen old palaces now inhabited by many families, convents transformed into schools, amphitheaters transformed into football fields; and such transforma-tions have always come about most effectively where neither an architect nor some shrewd administrator has intervened. Similarly, I recently heard a young man say that the eighteenth-century theater was a splendid form of collective house, in which the stage was the only private aspect of the building; and descriptions of eighteenth-century life, Stendhal's of La Scala for example, correspond with this insight.

This freedom of typology, once established, has always fascinated me as a problem of form. On this subject I could cite numerous examples, but I would be repeating things I have already said. Certainly I have always been enthu-siastic about the taverns set up under the huge arches of the Schnell-Bahn in Berlin, the two-story kiosks that sit behind the cathedral in Ferrara, and many other things where a particular function causes an event to unfold beneath the most unexpected roofs.

It is like the idea of sacredness in architecture: a tower is neither solely an image of power nor a religious symbol. I think of the lighthouse, the huge conical chimneys of the Castello di Sintra in Portugal, silos and smokestacks. The latter are among the most beautiful architecture of our time, but it would be untrue to say that they lack architectural models: this is another silly idea from modern or modernist criticism.

Man has always built with an aesthetic intention, and the great factories, docks, warehouses, and smokestacks of the industrial period had for models the worst Parisian architecture of the Beaux-Arts period. In this sense, few Europeans (although here Loos must be excluded) have understood the beauty of the American city and especially the beauty of New York.

America is certainly an important page in the scientific autobiography of my projects, even though I arrived there rather late in my career. Still, time prepares one in strange ways. While my early education was influenced by American culture, this influence occurred mostly through the cinema and literature; for me, American things were never "objects of affection." I am referring particularly to North American culture, since I have always viewed Latin America as a source of fantastic invention, and I used to consider myself, proudly and presumptuously, a Hispanophile.

Moreover, I could not respond with any first-hand experience to the descrip-tions, books, and images furnished by the architects of the American city. In fact, even when I was accused of being too immersed in books, especially as a boy, I was always concerned with the relation between study and direct experience. This is perhaps another reason that I have not completely lost my ties with Lombardy, and that I manage to mix, as it were, old sensations with new impressions.

In any case, I realized at a certain point that the official criticism of architec-ture had not included America or, what was worse, had not looked at it: the critics were preoccupied only with seeing how modern architecture had been transformed or applied in the United States. This also was connected with a vague anti-fascism, a search for the modern city, and many other beautiful things of which social-democratic culture has always sought examples without ever finding them.

Yet it is well known that in no place has modern architecture failed so badly as in the United States. If there is a transplant or transformation that ought to be studied, it lies in the great Parisian architecture of the Beaux-Arts period, in academic German architecture, and naturally in the most profound aspects of the English city and countryside—not to mention the Spanish Baroque architecture in Latin America, which offers a similar situation.

I believe that no city better than New York so plainly confirms the truth of the theses I set forth in *The Architecture of the City*. New York is a city of stone and monuments such as I never believed could exist, and on seeing it, I realized how Adolf Loos's project for the *Chicago Tribune* competition was his interpretation of America, and not of course, as one might have thought, a Viennese *divertissement*: it was his synthesis of the distortions created in America by an extensive application of a style in a new context. And the area which surrounds this city-monument is the entire vast territory of the country. Only in such a context does great architecture, the work of the masters, have value: it is the same in Venice, where although one may be interested in whether a building is by Palladio or Longhena, it is first and always the stones of Venice.

If I were to speak now of my American work or "formation," I would be digressing too far from the scientific autobiography of my projects and would be entering into a personal memoir or a geography of my experience. I will say only that in this country, analogies, allusions, or call them observations, have produced in me a great creative desire and also, once again, a strong interest in architecture.

For example, I found walking on Sunday mornings through the Wall Street area to be as impressive as walking through a realized perspective by Serlio or some other Renaissance treatise-writer. I have had a similar experience in the villages of New England, where a single building seems to constitute the city or village, independent of its size.

In 1978, when I was teaching at The Cooper Union, I gave my students the theme of the "American academical village." This theme interested me because it has many references in this culture which are truly foreign to Europeans: for example, the very concept of the "campus." The results of this assignment seemed extraordinary to me, because they rediscovered older themes and went back beyond the unique order of Thomas Jefferson's "academical village" to the architecture of forts, to the New World where the old was silence, above all.

These experiences, I repeat, like my stays in Argentina and Brazil, had a peculiar effect on me: while on the one hand they increasingly distracted me from my concentration on architecture, on the other they seem to have crystallized objects, forms, ideas about design.

It occurs to me that I now arrive at silence by a completely different route from that youthful method which grew out of purism: silence now seems to me an exact image, or superimposition, which in the end cancels itself out. It cancels itself out, that is, in the sense of this passage from St. Augustine: "All these things that are very good will come to an end when the limit of their existence is reached. They have been allotted their morning and their evening."

But perhaps we do not know when the moment of evening falls because a great mirror somewhere reflects architecture only as the place where life unfolds.

In Argentina I saw houses scattered at great distances along the Rio Paraná; they had small dock-like terraces floating on the great river and linked to the houses by landings. I visited the charming house called *dell' italiano*, one of the most beautiful places I have ever seen, built by a man who had come from a Europe that has since vanished from memory. Inside the house was the room of a poet who committed suicide, preserved with its white embroidered sheets, mirror, and flowers. It was all so remote that the reflection of the architecture in the mirror, as sometimes happens, recaptured the contours of the event in a timeless moment. The huge ships which passed on the river were not different in their marking of the time from the boats on the lake of my childhood.

Thus all I need do now is speak about a few of my projects, trying to order them according to this notion of quality. For with this scientific autobiography of my projects, I have not wholly given up the notion of writing a treatise, even if today the traditional order of the treatise has inevitably become a catalogue. And I often look attentively at such catalogues, but they do not interest me.

Our predecessors, on the other hand, considered questions of quality in their treatises; and Boullée's architecture of shadows and Palladio's search for place or *locus* are not merely autobiographies. For it is always the idea of place, and hence light and time and imagination, that recurs in the treatise-writers as that which can modify and finally be adapted in architecture. Even Guarini, in his obsession with mathematical rules, or precisely because of this obsession, observes that "we will be faithful to Vitruvius if in adapting ourselves to the requirements of a place we change the symmetries by adding to or subtracting from their correct proportions; thus it will become clear how much can be removed from them without harm in order to adapt to a site; as Vitruvius concludes: '*igitur statuenda est primum ratio Symmetriarum, a qua sumatur sine dubitatione commutatio* [therefore the first rule of the Symmetries should be stated as undoubtedly allowing for modification].'" It is from here, then, that the analysis of buildings proceeds: buildings are like a succession of opportunities to distance oneself from the original *ratio*, and this almost always happens, although clearly without the rule there can be no change.

Of course, the quality of all these things presupposes measurement. Yet how can one measure the size and quality of that sheer drop into space that I mentioned earlier in connection with a certain room? How can one measure the quality of Lord Jim's fall when it is a fall from which he will never rise again? How can one measure buildings, if an amphitheater can become a city, and a theater a house?

Thus when I here recount some of my projects, even repeating what I have written previously, there hardly seems to be any difference between the personal note and the description, between autobiography and technique, between what might be and what is not.

We could speak of every project as if it were an unfinished love affair: it is most beautiful before it ends.

And for every authentic artist this means the desire to remake, not in order to effect some change (which is the mark of superficial people) but out of a strange profundity of feeling for things, in order to see what action develops in the same context, or how, conversely, the context makes slight alterations in the action.

I am again approaching what I stated a moment ago about the theater and the mirror. The desire to remake something is similar to retaking the same photograph: no technique is ever sufficiently perfect to prevent changes introduced by the lens and the light, and in the end, there is always a different object anyway.

Certainly there is always a different object. This is perhaps what is autobiographical in a building and what I like to see in architecture, but also in the abandonment of architecture. For a past without the desire of the present is sad.

As I have said, *Forgetting Architecture* comes to mind as a more appropriate title for this book, since while I may talk about a school, a cemetery, a theater, it is more correct to say that I talk about life, death, imagination.

In speaking of these objects and projects of mine, I think once again of ending my work as an architect. It is a task that I have always attempted. I used to think that my last project, like the last known city, like the last human relationship, would be a search for happiness, identifying happiness with a sort of peace. Yet it may rather be the happiness of an intense but always definitive restlessness. As a result, every moment of becoming conscious of things is merged with a wish to be able to abandon them, to gain a sort of freedom that lies only in the experience of them, something like an obligatory rite of passage, which is necessary so that things might have their measure.

Yet certainly fulfillment goes beyond the work of architecture, and each object is only the first premise of what one would like to do. I have considered all this, gazing at the figure of Fortuna from a Venetian balcony, and yes, I thought, and still think, of the machine of architecture. This machine is in reality the machine of time.

In time and place I have found an analogy for architecture, what I have called "the fixed scene of human events." And this too has focused my interest on the theater and the *locus* it constitutes. I loved the fixed scene of the theater in Orange; somehow that great stage wall could not but be fixed. And the great amphitheaters of Arles, Nîmes, and Verona are also clearly delimited

23 Farmhouse near Parma.

and permanent places, since they were the *loci* of my architectural education. On Arles in particular I could write a study, a historical monograph or an architectural treatise, or simply a memoir. There I understood why Jean Genet declares that the architecture of the theater has yet to be discovered, although to me it is clear that the theater must be stationary, stable, and irreversible—but this seems true for all architecture.

Elements which are a mixture of the anomalous and the ordinary are pleasing to me; they can be glimpsed anywhere an unexplored landscape, a little-known geography of the city, arises in human events.

I read Bishop Palladio's[3] *Historia Lausiaca* and *The Life of St. Anthony*, and I was impressed by the monks' cities, the convents scattered across the desert, and farther out, the hermits' caves. Thousands of men lived in desert monasteries as in secret cities spread out over a sun-parched region. You can call these dimensions of time and space "architecture" as you call a monument architecture. I saw something similar in Puglia, near Lucera: it was a huge, practically inaccessible crater in which caves were dug out along the vertical walls, forming a forbidding amphitheater, burned by the rays of the sun yet at the same time cold. This was the place of anchorites, brigands, prostitutes, and *perdidos*, and it still produces this strange impression. I saw an ancient city that was an alternative to the history of civilization; it was a city that seemed to have no history: it consisted of its people's lives, rather than the consumption of their bodies and minds. But here too there were ruins, created by nature yet always constructed out of those living relationships that exist even in solitude—ruins not unlike those of Federico di Svevia's nearby castle, or of the plan of the Arabian city, or ruins which became confounded with each other, mingling regulating lines, profiles, human bodies, architectural materials. And I especially loved these vital places of the south: they are like the mysteries of Delphi and the mystery of time.

For this reason, ever since my childhood, saints' lives and mythological stories have shown me so many things disturbing to common sense that I have forever come to appreciate a certain spiritual restlessness, something latently bizarre in the order of life.

I have always known that architecture was determined by the hour and the event; and it was this hour that I sought in vain, confusing it with nostalgia, the countryside, summer: it was an hour of suspension, the mythical *cinco del la tarde* of Seville, but also the hour of the railroad timetable, of the end of the lesson, of dawn.

I loved the railroad timetable, and one of the books I have read most attentively is the timetable for the Swiss railroads. This is a volume written entirely in small, precious characters, where the world intersects the black typography, where trains, buses, steamers, and ferries carry us from east to west, and where a few pages, the most mysterious ones, contain places and distances shaded pale rose.

Thus they brought me again to the idea of analogy, which I have always

3. Born in Galatia in the late fourth century A.D., Bishop Palladio lived in Egypt and Palestine and served as the bishop of Helenopolis. His *Historia Lausiaca* (419 A.D.) is a collection of ascetics' lives.

regarded as the realm of probability, of definitions that approximated the object through a kind of cross-referencing. They intersected like train switches.

For my study of analogy, René Daumal's book *Mount Analogue* was enormously important, even if it only increased the anxiety of the search without telling me anything about its outcome. For a time I pursued the idea of analogy in mathematics and logic, and I still believe that mathematics alone offers a form of knowledge that gives satisfaction if not certainty, a kind of pleasure for its own sake, stronger and more detached than that of beauty or the moment.

Other than this I have found only disorder.

Perhaps Daumal's concept of analogy particularly struck me because of his comment about "the astounding speed of the already seen," which I connected with Ryle's definition of analogy as the end of a process. This book, in its ability to sum up my other readings and personal experiences, brought me to a more complex vision of reality, especially insofar as the conception of geometry and space was concerned. I encountered something similar to this in Juan de la Cruz's ascent of Mount Carmel: the representation of the mountain in his magnificent drawing/writing brought me back to my initial perception of the Sacri Monti, where the most difficult things to understand always seemed to me the meaning of and reason for the ascent. At around the same time as I was doing some research on Pavia with my students at the Politecnico in Milan, I came across Opicino De Canistris's map. In this map human and animal figures, sexual unions, and memories are confounded with the topographical elements of the relief; it demonstrates the different directions which art and science take at times.

All this was etched into my architecture and completely absorbed in everything I did: I read the geometry of the monuments at Cuneo and Segrate as derived from complex sources, even though others emphasized their purism and rationalism. And yet these sources have become clearer to me, just as whenever I draw a triangle I always think not only of the difficulty of closing it, but of the richness implicit in the error.

It must have been around 1968 that a general subversion of culture strangely revealed itself in my intellectual development. I recovered aspects of myself which had belonged to me in the past but which I had let fall into neglect. Hence in my notes on Daumal's book there is a passage from the tenth book of Plato's *Republic*, which in fact constituted a creative obsession for me, even though I do not recall ever having read it:
"After seven days spent in the meadow the souls set out again and came on the fourth day to a place from which they could see a shaft of light running straight through earth and heaven, like a pillar, in color most nearly resembling a rainbow, only brighter and clearer; after a further day's journey they entered this light and could then look down its axis and see the ends of it stretching from the heaven, to which they were tied; for this light is the tie rod of heaven which holds its whole circumference together like the braces of a trireme."
Above all, I was struck by the expression "they entered" and by the idea that there existed a point where one could enter, a point which had a relationship to this heavenly shaft of light, visible only from the ends of its reach. This

entering contains a beginning and an end; and without thinking more about this particular passage, years later I would come to linger over the meaning of the beginning and the end as values independent from the intermediate stages. I think that too many people dwell on the intermediate stages. Thus I have lost my interest in the catalogue, the collection, the botanical chart, because they have to do with that intermediate stage which I often find intolerable.

I love the beginning and end of things; but perhaps above all I love things which are broken and then reassembled, as in archaeological and surgical operations. Throughout my life I have often been hospitalized for fractures and other injuries to my bones, and this has given me some sense and knowledge of the engineering of the body, which would otherwise have been inconceivable to me.

Perhaps the only defect of the end, as well as the beginning, is the fact that it is partly intermediate. This is true because it can in some ways be foreseen. And of course the most foreseeable end is death.

I relate all this to my childhood impression of the prophet Elijah, to the memory of an image and an event. In large books full of Biblical stories, I used to look at the figures that issued from the dense, black text with their burning colors—yellows, blues, greens. A fiery chariot rose toward a sky that was crossed by a rainbow, and a great old man stood erect in it. As always, a very simple caption was printed under the illustration: "The prophet Elijah did not die. He was carried off by a fiery chariot." I have never seen such a precise representation and definition—almost never do events of this kind occur in fairy tales. The entire Christian religion is founded on death, deposition, and resurrection, and this is a most human iconography to represent man and god. In the disappearance of the prophet Elijah, I sensed something threatening to common sense, a challenge, an act of immense arrogance. But all this came close to satisfying my inclination for an act that was absolute and extremely beautiful. Perhaps I would later find part of this in Drieu La Rochelle, but the meaning was different.

I now believe that the beginning and end of things have been most important for me, and they have acquired much clarity: there is a close relationship between my initial search to reestablish the discipline of architecture and my final result of dissolving or forgetting it. It seems to me that modern architecture, as it originally presented itself, was a set of vague notions dominated by a secondhand sociology, a political deception, and a suspect aestheticism. The beautiful illusion of the Modern Movement, so reasoned and moderate, was shattered under the violent yet definitive collapse caused by the bombings of the Second World War. And I sought what was left not as though it were a lost civilization, but rather by pondering a tragic photograph of postwar Berlin where the Brandenburg Gate was still standing in a landscape of ruins. This was perhaps the victory of the avant garde; there are no longer any remains of the Frankfurt housing or of modern Dutch building intermixed with an amiable landscape from the time of Umberto I. Only among the ruins of these places did the avant garde win and lose: in the tangible surrealist landscape and the layers of rubble, which are certainly a gesture, although a destructive one. Not the architecture but the city of man was struck; and what was left certainly did not belong to architecture. It was rather a symbol, a sign, at times a tiresome memory.

82

Thus I have learned how to look at cities with an archaeological and surgical eye. I have disliked modernist aesthetics like any other formal revival, and as I have said, my early experience of Soviet architecture helped me to sweep away every petit-bourgeois inheritance of modern architecture. There remain for me a few great architects, like Adolf Loos and Mies van der Rohe, who pass substantially beyond social-democratic illusions.

To explain architecture in terms of the givens that are its proper domain means posing the problem in a scientific way, removing any superstructure, bombast, and rhetoric which encrusted it during the years of the avant garde. Such an explanation more than ever involves the dissolution of a myth and the reinsertion of architecture between the figurative arts and technology. A slim volume by Pier Luigi Nervi on reinforced concrete, containing studies on Roman domes, urban topography, and archaeology, showed me the city and architecture as one. I believe that today this connection has become increasingly clear, and that the study of architecture has found a greater credibility, provided this study is kept within the limits that are proper to it.

This also means dealing with disorder in some way, since it seems to correspond most closely to our state of mind. But I have always detested the arbitrary disorder that is an indifference to order, a kind of moral obtuseness, complacent well-being, forgetfulness.

And this has also meant knowing that the general condition must be experienced personally, often through small things, because the possibility of great ones has been historically precluded.

So I continue my architectural activity with the same persistence, and it seems to me that my vacillation between a rigid and historical geometry and the quasi-naturalism of objects may be a precondition for this type of work. Naturally, this vacillation is circumscribed by certain choices, which may include my first impressions of the Sacri Monti and my heightened interest in the theater and in a disturbing way of understanding history. This disturbing quality, or irritation as it has been called, has always characterized my designs in the eyes of those who have had to judge them or simply look at them.

Today I look at imitations of my projects which have been—how shall I put it?—well received, and they provoke in me a special interest, of a very different nature from the disdainful reaction of Picasso, who said something like, "You spend years making something, and then someone else comes along and makes it cute." I should talk about the nature of this interest or judgment of mine concerning what can be called plagiarism or else the copying of my work.

Yet it is no longer very important to me, and the copy is certainly intrinsic to the work itself.

In architecture as in the other technics, there exist precedents which have been handed down and which belong to architecture; there also exist copies of things which once were very personal, but these, if made by the best architects, are a token of affection and an authentic testimony. In any case, despite the critics, I judge affirmatively and lovingly every imitation of what I may call my own architecture, and I believe that on this subject I have nothing more to say.

I have nothing more to say because the matter is, so to speak, uncontrollable: the phenomenon of the transmission of thought or of what we call experience or of the world of forms is not connected to a program or a style and perhaps not even to a school. For this reason when I teach I always try to provide particulars and generally suggest a type of work that is sufficiently clear and almost reductive; I try not to provide models, but rather a technique on the one hand and an invitation to a broadening of knowledge on the other: analyzing the links which connect one's general and personal development to a certain technique has always seemed a mechanical operation to me, just like the practice of seeing autobiography only as the nexus of collective history and creation, even if we know that at specific moments these are superimposed and intermixed. Perhaps a parallel description, as I have tried to provide in this book, has value. On the other hand, certain of the authors I have cited here, such as Loos or Conrad, have entered my mind and virtually possessed it, whether or not they were architects, and these particular affinities and choices are part of my own development and my own mode of being.

I have thought of using this book to analyze my projects and writings in a continuous narrative sequence—understanding, explaining, and simultaneously redesigning them. Yet I have seen how, in writing all this down, one creates another project, which in itself contains something unforeseeable and unforeseen. I said that I have always liked things that were brought to a conclusion, and that every experience has always seemed conclusive to me: I have always felt that I was making something that would permanently exhaust my creativity. But always this possibility of conclusion has escaped me, even though an autobiography or an ordering of one's work might well be such a decisive occasion.

Other memories, other motives have come into view, modifying the original project which is still very dear to me.

Thus, this book is perhaps simply the history of a project, and like every project, it must be conclusive in some way, even if only so that it can be repeated with slight variations or displacements, or assimilated into new projects, new places, and new techniques—other forms of which we always catch a glimpse in life.

Drawings, Summer 1980

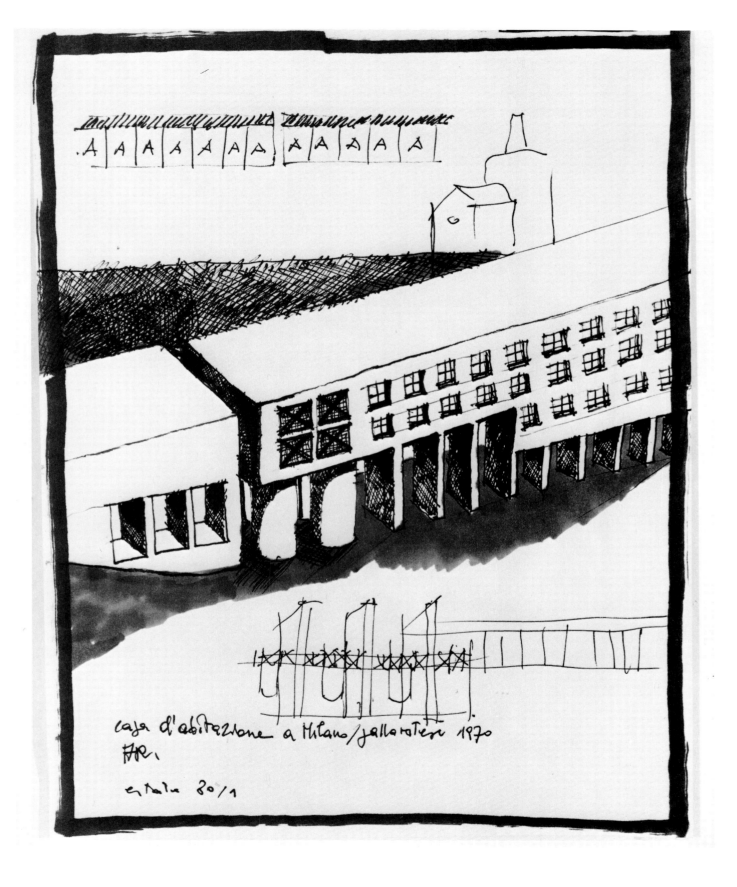

casa d'abitazione a Milano/gallaratese 1970
AR.

scala 80/1

Il monumento di
Segrate 1965
AR

estate 20/2

il cubo di Cuneo
HR 62

estate 80/3

4 Pile foundation for lighthouses
with theatre, 1980.

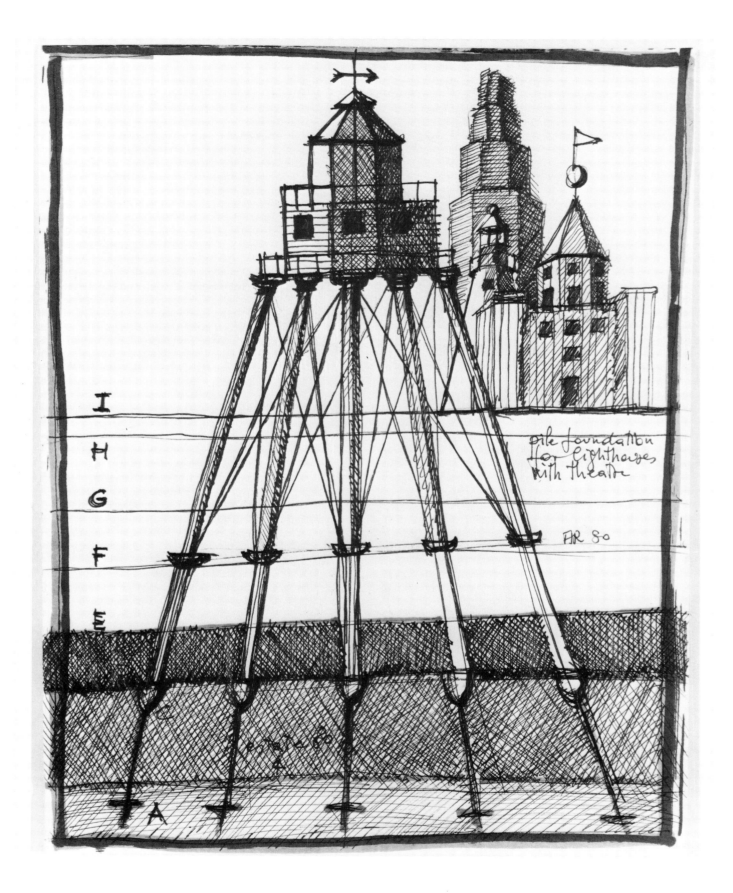

pile foundation
for lighthouses
with theatre

FYR 80

5 *Le cabine dell'Elba, 1975.*

le cabine dell'Elba
luglio AR 75

estate 80
5

*6 La casa dello studente di Chieti,
1976.*

La casa dello studente di Chieti
76 AR   estate 80 / 6

7 Le case sul Ticino, 1975.

8 Il portico di Modena, 1977.

Il ponte di Modena

estate 80 / 8

9 Le case di Bergamo, 1979.

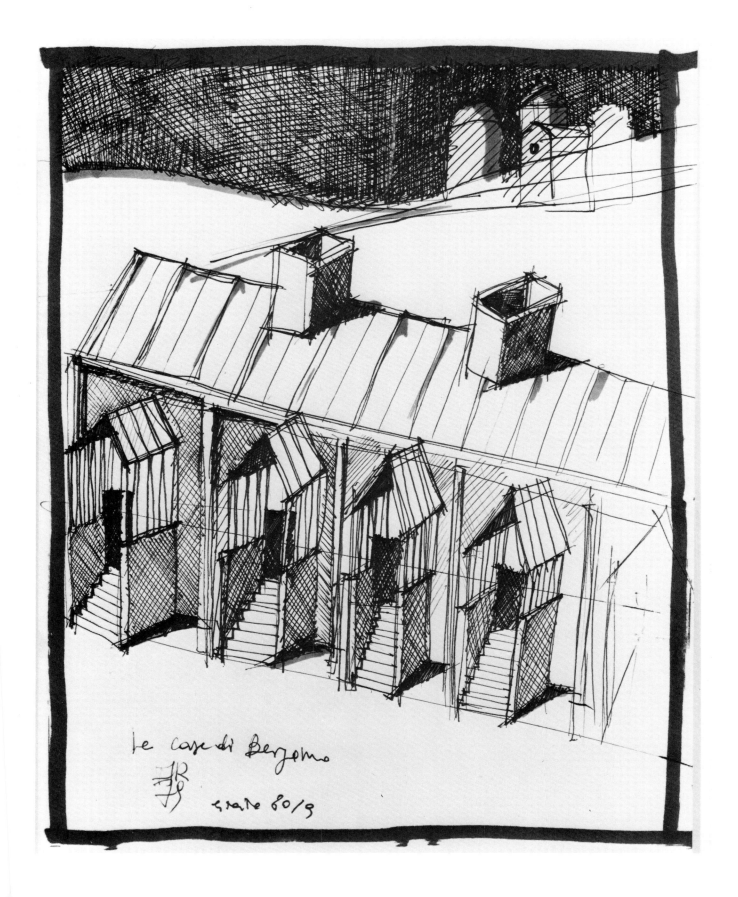

Le case di Bergamo

erase 80/9

10 La scuola di Broni, 1978.

La scuola di Bran

AR 78

a Pete 80/10

11 Teatro veneziano, 1979.

teatro veneziano 79   AR

arcate 80/11

12 Porta a Venezia, 1980.

porta a Venezia '8
AR
a la te 80/12

Postscript: Ideology in Form

Vincent Scully

For me this book has something of the quality of a divesting. When I finished reading it I felt utterly solitary, shorn of ideologies, alone with the memory of the things I have seen. It is not a linear book; it does not begin somewhere and get somewhere. It circles. So everything is dreamlike: changing but static, revolving around fixed points of obsession. Conscious reasoning seems left behind. Finally, there is only light, revealing objects; and every object, tower, or coffeepot has an identical being, the same scale. One feels that a great thing has happened, that Rossi has opened a white window onto sight. He has been able to divest himself of ideology almost entirely. Consequently there is no predetermined connection between things, no hierarchy. Everything is seen afresh, may be connected with other things in some new way. This is Rossi's greatest strength; it enables his eyes to focus upon the nonrational life of objects that may be said to go on inside the brain of man but is not identical with his reason. So the adjective "scientific" which Rossi employs takes on an ironic tinge but is deadly serious. Rossi did not start with this vision; no one does. His L'Architettura della città was a reasoned argument. Now there is something else; everything that impedes the irrationality of perception has been gone through, cast aside. In Italy Rossi must be infuriating as well as beloved. In the ferociously ideological ambience of so much North Italian criticism, where visual materials are commonly used only as approximate illustrations of conceptual positions, and are judged aesthetically according to the ideological justifications which may be assigned to them, it is a wonder to encounter a mind wherein the forms of art are so stubbornly innocent: pervasive, fragile, intransigently remembered.

Rossi is utterly clear on this major issue of memory throughout the text. His forms are few precisely because they are not made up but remembered. They derive from his experience of things in life. So he writes, "my observation of things has remained my most important formal education; later observation is transmuted into a memory of these things." So memory is a distillation, and Rossi's work suggests that his observed things are indeed idealized by it, "Platonized" into enduring shapes. But by definition, those shapes must derive originally from the culture in which Rossi grew up. They are in fact primarily North Italian in character, with an added Andalusian component, reflecting Rossi's special love for southern Spain. There is also, as for so many contemporary European intellectuals, some insistent American material. And all these memories can have a special life somewhere between thought and dimension because of Rossi's special talent as a draftsman—as, indeed, a painter. Rossi's drawings are often truly paintings, richly environmental and atmospheric, drenched in tonal washes and an often melancholy light. They explore the mysteries of remembrance, exactly as those of De Chirico did before them. Curiously, too, they have some of that sense of the ruin, or at least of the fragment, which so moved Piranesi, that other great architectural visionary; while the line drawings in particular tend to recall Vespignani's passionate recording of the modern ruins of half-built neighborhoods at the edges of Rome directly after the Second World War. The drawings are beyond all else spatial; they create architectural volumes and urban environments. They are not abstract studies but recordings of visions. Here Rossi's insistence upon architecture as a stage for human action sets an expectant tone; the spaces are taut with possibility, deeply evocative of presences as yet hidden but about to step forth, grand and melancholy like tragic actors on the classic stage. The drawings are therefore not schematic; they create the

illusion of environments to be populated—which is after all what
architecture is about. Another reason for their eminently architectural
character is their classical and vernacular background. They are dealing
with an Italy which has been built upon for more than two thousand years.
They are as open to the forms of light industry—one sees the little metal
factory sheds of the Po valley in them everywhere—as they are to the great
stuccoed masonry farms stretched out in the plain and the little wooden
huts clinging to the mountains of the north. All this is what one means by
vernacular—here a North Italian one. From this it naturally follows that
the remembered forms in the drawings are all fundamentally structural
ones, not structurally exhibitionistic like so many of the shapes of late
modernism, but recording the basic structural types of a vernacular both
peasant and industrial and reflecting always the pervasive classical past:
the masonry wall with its window voids, the massive column and lintel, the
wooden frame with diagonal bracing, the light metal skeleton, the great
truss in steel or timber, the gable shape, the cylindrical tower, the box, the
vault, the dome. These make Rossi's language never abstract, always
Italian.

Yet it is true that Rossi feels a movement in himself away from his "first
projects, where I was interested in purism" to a later concern for
"contaminations, slight changes, self-commentaries, and repetitions." This
seems to suggest a development in him from what might be called a
"modern" to a more "post-modern" position. But neither label is a good one
for Rossi. He rejects the first with enormous contempt, and he never
mentions the second, in which the relativistic pluralism of so much of post-
modern theory would of course be wholly foreign to him. It is not "cultural
coding" that moves and directs him but a more ancient faculty, one which
may properly be identified with Mnemosyne (Memory), the essential
goddess of the classical aestheticians. It is she, the mother of the Muses,
who is invested with the function of analogical transformation, which Rossi
sometimes claims as the very soul of his work—and sometimes claims to
have discarded. Mnemosyne is that sheaf of memories which shapes the
aesthetic faculty—the capacity to sift, choose, and distinguish, and from
which all her daughters derive. Since the workings of that process are a
mysterious affair, Mnemosyne is divine, not to be taken lightly. At first,
Rossi tries to hold her at bay. "I began these notes about ten years ago," he
writes, "and I am trying to conclude them now so that they do not turn into
memories." He hopes instead—acting out of another pervasive
Mediterranean instinct, its sculptural one—to sustain a sense of the present
as absolute. "Every summer seemed to me my last summer, and this sense
of stasis without evolution may explain many of my projects." But as the
text goes on the barriers between Rossi and his memories progressively fall
away. They are an ocean of remembered shapes; finally they all flood in
and range themselves classically for his use. "Now I seem to see all the
things I have observed arranged like tools in a neat row; they are aligned as
in a botanical chart, or a catalogue, or a dictionary. But this catalogue,
lying somewhere between imagination and memory, is not neutral; it
always reappears in several objects and constitutes their deformation and,
in some way, their evolution."

And he adds, as if sheepishly, "I believe that it may be difficult for the critic
to understand all this from outside." But he is really letting the critic in:
beyond discourse, sharing the movements of his mind. Instantly he feels

112

liberated to pass on to Melville's vision, cited by poet Charles Olson, and wholly descriptive of his own grandest forms: "Light house & monastery on bold cliff. Cross. Cave underneath light house. The whole Atlantic breaks here. Lovely afternoon." From that point on for Rossi it is all "happiness"— "summer"—"idiocy"—"astonishment." He has dealt with Death before, a point to which we must return. So all forms become innocent. Somewhere, as he says, "between fascism and idiocy," they are resemanticized into a fresh language. Out of animal being. In the famous drawing of L'architecture assassinée *they are small, eager creatures in a state of massacre, slashed across the forehead, machine-gunned in the legs: stood up against the wall by ideology.*

Rossi is innocent. That innocence is hard won, valiant. He too risks massacre because now he trusts his forms, stands with them. No text before his has so reminded me of Henri Focillon's luminous Vie des Formes *of 1934.[1] There Focillon says of art, "It must renounce thought, must become dimensional . . . It creates an image of the world that has nothing in common with the world, and an art of thinking that has nothing in common with thought." This is Rossi's way. Again he is no more verbally than conceptually systematic but follows that other logic of things. For Focillon too forms led their own lives: "within this great imaginary world of forms, stand on the one hand the artist and on the other hand form itself. Even as the artist fulfills his function of geometrician and mechanic, of physicist and chemist, of psychologist and historian, so does form, guided by the play and interplay of metamorphoses, go forever forward, by its own necessity, toward its own liberty."*

So it does for Rossi. And with this he becomes a great architect. We can watch the process taking place in his drawings. Hence he despises functionalist theory and the mechanical determination of so much of the Modern Movement. Indeed, he is harder on modernism than are most post-modern critics, who tend now to regard it as simply another style. Rossi sees it as a contemptible enemy: hypocritical, sentimental, moralizing, full of slipshod justifications on a "petty bourgeois" level. His projects and buildings are therefore intended "not, as the functionalists thought, because they carry out a determined function, but because they permit other functions. Finally, because they permit everything that is unforeseeable in life."

So form, because it follows not function but a logic other than that of human reason, can liberate that reason and the life it directs. For Rossi, though, it liberates through its very limitation. As we have noted, Rossi's forms are few and carefully selected out of his memories— self-selected, one might say, through their persistence in that memory. This is another reason for their dreamlike quality, since each one indirectly stands for so many things: for every gable, every column, every tower, saint, and flag. In order to do so they must be geometrically simplified, must indeed give the impression of being abstract while not actually being so at all. Here again, as with Frank Lloyd Wright, it is a matter of simplification as "indirect representation," escaping the conscious censor like the pictorial embodiments of Freud's dream work. Out of this, as we have seen, Rossi's forms create a dream-Italy unmatched since De Chirico's time. And from this their relationship with Fascist forms derives. The Fascists consciously intended to reinvoke the classical and vernacular traditions of Italian architecture and to make them their own. Modern architecture, with its contempt for the

1. *Translated by George Kubler and C.B. Hogan as* The Life of Forms in Art *(New Haven, 1942; new ed. New York, 1948).*

113

vernacular and the monumental alike, was in the end powerless to sustain itself against those forms. Hence, as in the great square of Milan, the Fascists seized the center of the cities with their monuments, while those of the Modern Movement—like the touching little memorial of the BBPR to the dead Gian Luigi Banfi—found their place in the suburbs, precisely because they were incapable of dealing with the large, timeless, symbolic themes that shape communal human life. Modern architecture lost to Fascism. Rossi retakes the city. He can do so because he is better at it than the Fascist architects were. He regains the tradition more vitally because he is operating through memory rather than ideology. One of those memories is of modern architecture itself, through and beyond which Rossi is in fact seeing the classical past. That, once apparently worn out, is thus perceived afresh and so revitalized, and can begin again in a primitive phase, with a primitive strength. Fascism too is part of the memory now, and haunts it, and indeed endows Rossi's forms with much of their special physical and associational aura.

Fascism haunts the colonnade of the Gallaratese project, but it is only one of the ghosts. Every classical architect from Le Corbusier to Ledoux and Ictinos is lurking behind the piers. All of Italy is there in public grandeur and private poverty and indomitable rhetorical stance. An American cannot fail to guess that Louis Kahn is also present. His majestic drawing of the hypostyle hall at Karnak—where the columns are neither structurally muscular nor sculpturally active but simply enormously there, modeling the light, taking up space—seems almost prototypical of Rossi's colossal columns here. These are so big in relation to their modest load that there seems to be no structural compression upon them and they remain purely visual beings, apparitions stepping forward among the flat piers. Whatever the case, the colonnade of the Gallaratese is the ultimate space of dream. Judged by the functionalist criteria of modernist criticism it might be seen as over-scaled and gratuitous, but it must in fact be seen literally in another light, in that of Rossi's "unforeseeable functions." And there, however relegated to the edges of consciousness, its shapes march through the corridors of sleep and populate dreams. It is only fair to Freud to note that there may well be a sexual element in this as well, since the long, taut shape of Rossi's slab is clearly read as a body intruding into Aymonino's brown, ebullient, L-shaped building. Whatever the reasons, and they are surely many, something deep is touched, some need of the soul for space and grandeur, for glory, love, and connection, some generous wish not verbalized but pictorially represented here.

The same is true of the cemetery at Modena, where the wish is for death, Freud's "third casket," so beautiful is it seen to be, so unforseeable in its promise. Some of Rossi's most moving paragraphs have to do with his experience at Modena, which was put together out of the ache in his broken bones. He tells us how he turned the problem over in his mind as he lay in a hospital bed far away in the Balkans and began to build Modena up as a bone structure, a city of bone, built of bone, housing bone. This kind of death was the end of his youth, he tells us, but after it came that "happiness," that "idiocy" of joy in life we noted before. As such a rite of passage, the design of Modena brings together a richer assemblage of memories than does any other of Rossi's works. It is the most Romantic-Classical. Boullée, whom he translated and loved, is there. It is also the most Surrealist. De Chirico, whom he hardly ever mentions, certainly shapes this dream as

114

well. The house of life for Italy, the great palazzo block, becomes its house of death, without roof or window frames of interior floors. It is stripped of everything except its enduring masonry bones, recalling those of the Fascist monument to Italian culture at the EUR in Rome. Most of all, the glass of the Modern Movement is wholly cast aside, as is all its canonical lightness, its taut surfaces and floating planes.

In all this, too, Americans cannot help but think of Louis Kahn once more. His famous "ruins," devoid of glass, which culminate in the timeless masses of Ahmedabad and Dacca, come immediately to mind. They are masonry structures pierced by pure voids and so simplified and abstractly scaled as to be suggestive of functions not specific but "unforseeable." They, too, seem Neoplatonic in their circles and squares. All these qualities are recalled at Modena, but they—if indeed they were "memories" for Rossi—are "transmuted" by Rossi's special gift for scenography into a noble terrain for the representation of death, a space grander than Mussolini's Forum, which Kahn also drew. Here Rossi's insistence upon the importance of the theater for his work seems especially relevant. He shows us that the architecture which he regards primarily as a setting for human action can create a theater even for death. Even the stillness of the dead is dramatized, and thus humanized, by it.

It is no wonder that Rossi's drawings and paintings having to do with Modena, which here as elsewhere tend to be more colorful, crowded, and tumultuous than the actual project, are among his most monumental and haunting. Like countless Italians before him, he is dreaming of the timeless city which is the habitation of the dead. There is, I think, nothing mysterious or morbid in this, since the city is the place where living men normally come into closest contact with their ancestors who shaped the city before them. For the Hopi of the Southwest the god of the pueblo is Masau'u, the god of death. And the city of the dead itself plays a special part in the life of Italy; it stands outside the gates of Tarquinia, Cerveteri, Rome, and Pompeii. So ancient Etruscan divinities are embodied in the awesome cone which culminates Modena, no less than are the cenotaph of Boullée, De Chirico's sad chimneys, and the ovens of Dachau. All terrors of the passage are thus transmuted by the order of the city, where all sleep together at last, bone in bone.

The linear habitations carried on flat piers at Modena return in the Gallaratese but are now lifted as well by the life in the full, round columns, which are indeed the life-giving element of the whole. In one of the most comprehensive of the drawings which he based on Modena, Rossi shows us all these monumental forms but draws a sequence of another type across the lower left of the composition. It is a series of little houses with sharp-pointed frontal gables. Here Rossi's memory of the bathing pavilions of Elba comes into play. He draws them as skittering little shapes, their gables pierced by round windows, like vernacular echoes of the great oculus by Alberti at Mantua, which Rossi also illustrates in this book. Then the gable as a form reminiscent at once of the vernacular shack and the classical pedimented temple appears as a Platonic triangle in Rossi's monument for the partisans at Segrate. This conjunction also illustrates the essential difference between Rossi's design and that of his teacher and friend, the modern architect Ernesto Rogers. Rogers's monument to Banfi, which we mentioned earlier, is wholly nonmonumental and nondirectional; it is an affair of floating planes which purposely lack any reference to massive stabilities or to traditions either classical or vernacular. Rossi's project lunges; it also embodies monumental mass and direction and suggests the two traditions It thus employs all the traditional architectural strengths which the other avoids. It is a monument to human decision and belonging; the other a comment on human separateness and defeat.

Vernacular too are the crossed mullions in square windows which Rossi has come to use almost exclusively, as in his school at Fagnano Olona and his Teatro del Mondo at Venice. The same window has also been an essential element in the work of Robert Venturi, as in his Trubek and Wislocki houses in Nantucket. In each case, the Italian and the American, it is a question of a vernacular element (the cross-mullioned window is a standard nineteenth-century type) which has been distilled into a square form of arresting iconic power: the window as void, barrier, eye. When combined, as it more or less is in each instance, with a sharp gable, the sense of a continuity of intention and method between the two architects in question— previously considered polar opposites—grows strong. Each has been able to see, perceive, and remember the vernacular forms of his own culture and hence to break out of modern "design" to something deceptively more simple, even abstract, but in fact more traditional, basic, and enduring.

The great architecture of this generation may therefore be "International" once again, in a way which the architects of the International Style had never imagined. But there is no one comparable to Rossi for the kind of pure affection which he now seems able to embody in his forms. The Teatro del Mondo is the best example of this so far, though the play-monumental medieval gate for the Biennale of 1980 is not far behind it. For the Teatro the process begins once again with memory. The Baptistry of Florence is transmuted by it into a tower of touchingly primitive aspect, sheathed in wood, as by someone for whom that material suggested a source of not quite rustic but surely archaic power. Inside, a tubular steel structure like the memory of a skeletal pier frames a high vertical space like that of a Russian church, an elongated version of Shakespeare's Globe, il mondo, *the ultimate theatrical environment. Floating on its barge, the tall tower lifts and falls with the tide, its steel skeleton moving within the wooden sheathing, the whole body high-shouldered, narrow, and precarious like a Zuni Shalako bird. It, too, is a creature, with square, cross-mullioned eyes, but it is also Florence come to call in Venice, the Baptistry with its holy water now floating on the sea, its blue conical roof with globe and pennant riding gently up to the domes and globes of the Salute and Dogana del Mare.*

These forms all move to a kind of familiar affection because they seem to present us with a fundamental state of being, outside fashion, and calling into question even the concept of style, far more than the International Style ever did. They are forms which appear to be, as Rossi hoped, "without evolution." They simply are, as if they always were. Therefore they shun linguistic gestures. They are silent. Kahn, too, late in life, had called for "silence," and Rossi repeatedly states in this text that he wants his building to be "mute." He employs the German word sprachlos *to describe them. And speechless they stand, vehicles of remembrance, touching as in some physical faculty beyond the realm of words. Speechless, we open our hearts to them, and they guard our dreams.*

116

Biographical Note

Aldo Rossi's writings are intimately connected with his designs and architectural plans, which have been widely exhibited in Europe and America. His major built works include the residential complex in the Gallaratese 2 section of Milan, the elementary school of Fagnano Olona in the province of Varese, and the Teatro del Mondo in Venice. In 1977 Rossi was Mellon Professor at The Cooper Union, and he has taught at The Institute for Architecture and Urban Studies and Yale University. He currently teaches at the Istituto Universitario di Architettura in Venice.